Digital Administration

Digital Administration

Dr. Sunil Laxman Gawande

GenNext Publication

Published by

GenNext Publication
5, Ansari Road
Daryaganj, New Delhi-110002
Phone: 011-47034999, 9811692060
E-mail: gennextpublication@hotmail.com

Distribution Network
gyanbooks.com
India, USA, Canada, UK, Australia, France

ISBN: 978-93-5722-609-7 (PB)

First Published, 2024

Printed at: Gyan Press, Delhi.

DIGITAL ADMINISTRATION

Author: Dr. Sunil Laxman Gawande

Contents

Preface

In the 21st century, the rapid evolution of technology has transformed every aspect of our lives, including how governments and organizations operate. The concept of digital administration is no longer just an innovative idea; it has become an essential element for ensuring efficiency, transparency, and accountability in both public and private sectors. This book aims to explore the profound impact of digital technologies on administrative practices and to offer insights into how these technologies can be leveraged to improve governance and organizational management.

The journey toward digital administration is not without challenges. Issues such as data security, digital literacy, and the integration of legacy systems pose significant obstacles. However, the potential benefit such as streamlined processes, improved citizen services, and enhanced decision-making capabilities far outweigh these challenges. This book seeks to provide a comprehensive guide to navigating these complexities, offering practical solutions and strategic frameworks for successful digital transformation.

In the following chapters, we will delve into various facets of digital administration, including the principles of e-governance, the role of CSC and Setu Suvidha Kendra, the importance of cyber security, and the impact of artificial intelligence on administrative functions. Each chapter is designed to equip administrators, policymakers, and students with the knowledge and tools necessary to adapt to the digital era.

This book is the culmination of extensive research and collaboration with experts in the field of digital administration. I hope it serves as a valuable resource for those looking to understand and implement digital strategies within their organizations. The digital revolution is here, and it is imperative that we embrace it to build more efficient, responsive, and resilient administrative systems.

This book is designed to serve as a guide for policymakers, public administrators, academics, and anyone interested in the intersection of technology and governance. It presents case studies, best practices, and theoretical frameworks that illustrate the potential of digital governance to enhance public sector efficiency and citizen satisfaction.

Thank you for embarking on this journey with me. Together, we can explore the future of administration in the digital age.

- Dr. Sunil Laxman Gawande

Acknowledgement

The present book entitled, Digital Administration is based on my Post-Doctoral research. Among the people who encouraged me to complete this research and write the book, my post-doctoral research guide Prof. Dr. Panchasheel Ekambekar, principal, Late Bapusaheb Patil Ekambekar College, Hanegaon, Tq. Degloor Dist. Nanded. Also Prof. S.M. Varma, Director, ICSSR, New Delhi and all his staff

I express my utmost respect and gratitude to Prof. Nagarjun Wadekar, Director, School of Humanities and Social Sciences, Yashwantrao Chavan Open University, Nashik For his constant encouragement, valuable guidance and unending assistance. Despite his busy schedule in various education work, he was always available for me to reach out to whenever, I am grateful to his for the help and support needed.

I would like to convey a deep sense of gratitude to Dr. Charru Malhotra Department of e-governance & ICT Indian Institute of Public Administration, New Delhi. And Dr. Rashmi Anand, Research Officer, IIPA, New Delhi for her prompt help and direction. She always remained concerned about progress of my book writing work. I am very much thanking to Prof. Dr. D.M. Tangalwad, Academic Director, Mahatma Gandhi Antarrashtriy Vishavvidyalaya, Wardha for guiding and always encouraging me for research work and also my life.

I also thanks to Dr. Vijay Tarode, Dr. Anant Kousdikar, Dr. Kavita Sonkamble, Dr. Meera Phad, Dr. B. R Katturwar, Dr. Lekhane Shankar, Prof. Dr. Sanjay Bhalerao for their guidance and support always during this writing work and librarians various Institutes like, YCMOU, Nashik, SRTM University, Nanded, YASHADA Pune, IIPA, New Delhi. Also grateful to the officers related of revenue Department and operators of Digital services centre for their co-operation and support me.

I would like to thanks my friends Prof. Chandrakant Taru, Dr. Bhagwan Waghmare, Prof. Gangadhar Aklod, Prof. Gangadhar chavan, Dr. Smita Marwalikar, Dr. Markhale Shankar, Dr. Vadaje, Dr. Sanjay Khrat, Dr. Vijapure, all this friends co-operating me.

I am special thanks to my Dear wife Suchitra Gawande, she always co-operating in translation and typing for this writing work.

I deeply appreciate with many thanks, the support of my family members who encouraged me for this writing work and helped me.

I would like to thank all the people who have helped me both directly and indirectly during the period of this work.

- Dr. Sunil Laxman Gawande
drsunilgawande14@gmail.con

List of Abbreviations

Sr. No.	Abbreviations	Details
1.	ACA	Additional Central Assistance
2.	AEPS	Aadhar enable payment system
3.	ASPA	American Society for Public Administration
4.	ATIs	Administrative Training Institutes
5.	B2G	Business-to-government
6.	BBNL	Bharat broadband Network
7.	BBPCU	Bhart Bill Payment Central Unit
8.	BHIM	Bharat Interface for Money
9.	BPR	Business Process Re-engineering
10.	C2C	Consumer-to-consumer
11.	C2G	Citizens to government
12.	CAS	Common Application Software
13.	CBS	Cell Broadcasting Services
14.	CCEA	Cabinet Committee on Economic
15.	CCTV	Closed Circuit Television
16.	CCTYS	Crime and Criminal Tracking Network System
17.	C-DAC	Centre for Development of Advanced Computing
18.	CFC	Common facilities Centre
19.	CMP	Common Minimum Program
20.	COIS	Collectors Information System
21.	CSCs	Common Service Centre's
22.	CTI	Computer-telephone integration
23.	CTOs	Chief Technology Officers
24.	CVC	Central Vigilance Committee
26.	DARPG	Department of Administrative Reforms and Public Grievances

27.	DBT	Direct to benefits
28.	DeitY	Department of Electronics and Information Technology
29.	DFSS	Design for Six Sigma
30.	DI	Digital India
31.	DIOs	District Informatics officers
32.	DISHA	Digital Saksharta Abhiyan
33.	DIW	Digital India Week
34.	DoT	Department of Telecom
35.	DPR	Detailed Project Report
36.	DSL	Digital subscriber line
37.	DVD	Digital versatile disc
38.	e GAF	e-Government Assessment Framework
39.	E Governance	Electronics Governance
40.	E KYC	Electronic know your costumer
41.	EDI	Electronic Data Interchange
42.	EFC	Expenditure Finance Committee
43.	e-GAF	e-Governance Assessment Framework
44.	e-GCF	e-Governance Competency Framework
45.	EGDI	e-Government Development Index
46.	e-GPLC	e-Governance Project Life Cycle
47.	e-IDM	Electronic Identity Management
48.	EMS	Electronic Manufacturing Services
49.	EPIC	Electoral Photo ID Card
50.	EPL	e-Participation index
51.	ESDM	Electronics system design and manufacturing
52.	ETL	Extract, Transform, and Load
53.	FBS	Fixed Budget Selection
54.	FRS	Functional Requirements Specifications
55.	FSD	Functional Specification Document
56.	FSD	Functional Specification Document
57.	FSSAI	Food Safety and standards authority of India
58.	G2B	Government to Business
59.	G2C	Government to Citizens
60.	G2C2G	Government to Citizen to Government

61.	G2G	Government to Government
62.	GIS	Geo-Spatial Information System
63.	GoI	Government of India
64.	GOs	Government Orders
65.	GPR	Government process Re-engineering
66.	GPS	Global positioning system
67.	GST	Good and Service Tex
68.	ICT	Information and communication technology
69.	ICT4D	ICT for Development
70.	IFC	Information and Facilitation Counters
71.	IIPA	Indian Institute of public Administration
72.	IMWG	Inter Minister Working Group
73.	IoT	Internet and things
74.	IS	Information System
75.	ISO	International Organization for Standardization
76.	IT	Information Technology
77.	JAM	Jandhan, Aadhar, Mobile
78.	KPI	Key performance Indicators
79.	LAN	Local Area Network
80.	LBS	Location Based Services
82.	LCS	Location Based Services
83.	LDAP	Lightweight Directory Access Protocol
84.	MAN	Metropolitan Area Network
85.	MMPs	Mission mode Projects
86.	MMPs	Mission Mode- Project
87.	MMT	Mobile Money transfer
88.	MOOCS	Massive Open Online Course
89.	MOU	Memorandum of Understanding
90.	MSDG	Mobile Service Delivery Gateway
91.	MSDG	Mobile Service Delivery Gateway
92.	NCSP	National Cyber Security Policy
93.	NDLM	National Digital Literacy Mission
94.	NDSAP	National Data Sharing and Accessibility Policy
95.	NE	North East
96.	NeGD	National e-Governance Division

97.	NeGP	National e-Governance Plan
98.	NGOs	Non-Government Organizations
99.	NIC	National Informatics Centre
100.	NIC	National Informatics Centre
101.	NICSI	National Informatics Centre Service Inc.
102.	NKN	National Knowledge Network
103.	NLP	Natural Language Processing
104.	NNRMS	Natural Resources Management System
105.	NOFN	National Optical Fibre Network
106.	NPCI	National Optical Fibre Network
107.	NPI	National Portal of India
108.	NPIT	National Policy on Information Technology
109.	NRDMS	National Resources Date Management System
110.	NRIS	National Resources Information System
111.	NSDI	National Spatial Data Infrastructure
112.	NSDI	National Spatial Data Infrastructure
113.	NSDL	National security depository limited
114.	ODM	Original Design Manufacturers
115.	OGD	Open Government Date
116.	ONF	Open Networking Foundation
117.	OSS	Open Source Software
118.	P2P	Peer-to-Peer net working
119.	PaaS	Platform as a Service
120.	PKI	Public Key Infrastructure
121.	PLAPs	Public Internet Access points
122.	PMAY	Pradhan Mantri Awas Yojana
123.	PMKVY	Prdhan Mantri Kaushalya vikas Yojana
124.	PPP	Public Private Partnership
125.	PPR	Public Sector Process Rebuilding
126.	PRIs	Panchayati Raj Institutions
127.	PRSG	Project Review and Steering Group
128.	QBS	Quality Based Selection
129.	QCBS	Quality and Cost based Selection
130.	QMS	Quality Management System
131.	RAHI	Road and highways Information System

132.	RFP	Request for Proposal
133.	RSS	Real Simple Syndication
134.	RTE	Right to Education
135.	RTI	Right to Information
136.	SaaS	Software as a Service
137.	SADM	Software assessment of disability Maharashtra
138.	SARITA	Stamped Registration information technology administration
139.	SC/ST	Scheduled Caste/Scheduled Tribe
140.	SDC.	State Data Centre
141.	SDN.	Software Defined Network
142.	SEDG	State services Delivery Gateway
143.	SETU	Self-employment and talent utilization
144.	SLA	Service Level Agreement
145.	SLO	Service Level Objective
146.	SMAC	Social Media, Mobile, Analytics, Cloud
147.	SMAC	Social, Mobility, Analytics and Cloud
148.	SMART	Specific, Measurable, Achievable, Realistic and Time Bound
149.	SMART	Simple, Moral, Accountable, Responsible, Transparent
150.	SOA	Service-oriented Architecture
151.	SOAP	Service Oriented Architecture Protocol
152.	SOE	Service Oriented e-Governance
153.	SRS	System Requirements Specification
154.	SRS	System Requirements Specification
155.	STQC	Standardization testing and quality certification
156.	SWAN	State Wide Area Network
157.	ToTs	Training Of Trainers
158.	UDDI	Universal Description, Discovery, and Integration
159.	Umang	Unified Mobile Application for new age governance
160.	UPI	Unified Payment Interface
161.	URI	Uniform Resource Indicator
162.	USN	Ubiquitous Sensor Network
163.	USOF	Universal Service Obligation Fund

164.	USSD	Unstructured Supplementary Service Data
165.	UTS	Union Territory State
166.	VLES	Village Level Enter pinners
167.	WAN	Wide Area Network
168.	Wi- Fi	Wireless fidelity
169.	WSAN	Wireless Sensor Area Networks
170.	WSDL	Web Services Description Language

Chapter - 1

Introduction

"A transparent smart Digital governance with access secure and authentic flow of information crossing the interdepartmental barrier and providing a fair and unbiased service to the citizen."

Dr. A P J Abdul Kalam

The twentieth century is known as Knowledge based society and the age of science technology and information media and revolution in technology has its effect every sphere of human life. Good Governance is the key to Nation's progress and an important step towards it is the simplification of procedures and processes in the Government so as to make the entire system transparent and faster. Further; the ever expanding provision of citizen-centric online services is one of the most important aspects of an efficient and effective public Administration system as it leads to transparency and accountability in governance and als o fosters equitable growth. Technology is thus, both an empowering tool for citizens and a measure of accountability for the government. further, it is important to note that the vision of the Hon'ble prime Minister is the emphasis on ''Minimum Government and Maximum Governance.[1]

Minimum Government; Maximum Governance' is a key aspect of New India 2022 closely related to this is the growth of e-Governance through Unique and cutting edge initiative's in India. especially in the last few year with advancement in Information and Communication Technology (ITC) it has become possible to provide many public services through online mode in accordance with the estimates made by the National e – Governance Division (NEGD) of the department of Electronics and Information Technology (Deity) there are more than 3500 different e-services being offered by various central Ministers and state Government as per NIC estimates more than 8000 different portals and websites of central Ministers and state Governments are hosted by them.[2]

Today's world of change and revolution things which are not dynamic are considered as mortal the rise of e- Government has been one of the most striking developments of the web Global shifts towards increased deployment of it by government emerged in the nineties with the advent of the world wide web. The technology as well as e-Governance initiative have come a long way since them. Recognizing the increasing importance of electronics. The Government of India established the department of electronics in 1977.[3]

The subsequent establishment of the National Informatics center (NIC) in 1977 was the first major step toward e-Governance in India as it brought information and its communication in focus .However, the main trust for e-Governance was provided by the launching of NicNET in 1987 the National satellite based computer network this was followed by the launch of the District information system of the national Informatics center (DISNIC) to computerized all District offices in country for which free hardware and software was offered to the state Government.

E-Governance was started in India by AKSHAYA in Kerala. Kerala India's first digital state in February 2016,[4] former presidents Pranab Mukherjee declared Kerala as the first digital state of India owing to its achievement of high e-literacy and mobile penetration. It was also the first state to complete the National optical fiber Network (NOFN) project granting high speed Internet access to all its Grampanchyats.

India's First digital village, Akodara, is located in Gujarat.[5] The Government of Gujarat partnered with ICICI Bank which adopted the village and Converted it into a working model for Digital India from setting up bank accounts and going cashless to installing CCTV cameras, the village is a perfect example of what a digital village would look like.

To address all these deficiencies, the Department of Electronics and Information Technology, Government of India approved the National e-Governance plan (NEGP) in 2006.

National e-Governance plan (NEGP)

The Government of India approved the National e-Governance plan on 18th May, 2006 with a vision statement "make all Government services accessible to the common man in his locality; through common services delivery outlets and ensure efficiency, Transparency and reliability of such services at affordable cost to realize the basic needs of the common man.[6] NEGP lays emphasis on developing the proper governance and institutional Framework within India, established the ICT infrastructure and implement a various

Mission Mode project (MMPs) at the state central and integrated levels NEGPS aims and Moto is **'Ek kadam aapaki oar, Ek kadam aapake Liye.'** Public closer home NEGP consisting originally of 27 MMPs and components, during July 2011, 4 new MMPs were added.

The National Democratic Alliance (NDA) Government in India has recently introduced the new Concepts of 'Digital India' 'Make in India' to provide better facilities to the people through E-Governance and Administration the concepts of 'Digital India' has made a district change in the administration of Maharashtra. Today all the Government services from parliament to Grampanchyat are provided through E-Governance online.

Digitalization is one of the most fundamental period of transformation we have ever witnessed Digital India was a flagship program launched by the Prime Minister of India Narendra Modi on 1st July 2015[7] with an objective of connecting rural areas with high speed Internet Network and improving digital literacy of this program is to transform India into a digitally empowered society and knowledge economy it is one of the biggest steps by government of India to motivate the citizen of the country and connect Indian economy to Knowledge savvy world.

The society is changing rapidly hence there is a need of rapid development in the information and technology. The Government is ready to involve its citizen in the administration by providing them digital information technology and Government is also trying to keep transparency is its administration through Digital India .Digital India is a comprehensive approach which helps the Government to provide basic needs to the last citizen of the country. It provides basics needs to the last citizen of the country. It provides the opportunity to fulfill the objective of the social and economical development of the citizen. Government has included many schemes in its budget of 2017-2018 to promote Digital India programme as well as digital payment, Internet and optical fiber networking; Government has also made resolution in its budget to provide high speed broad band services, Hotspots through optical fiber to all the Grampanchyats. Hence in the recent future India is going to 'Digital India'[8]

Digital Maharashtra

Maharashtra is the pioneer state in the adoption of technology that supplements improvement in transparency and accountability of the Government the Maharashtra state is the pioneer in citizen, centric e-Governance initiatives like common services center, Maha e-seva, setusuvidha Kendra, Mahaonline, Aaplesarkar portal, Public Distribution system (PDS) Land record etc.

Maharashtra state E-Governance policy

Maharashtra is the first state in the country to have a dedicated e-governance policy published on 23 September, 2011[9] in local language i.e. Marathi and also English language. The policy's aims to maintain and strengthen the leadership of the state in the area of e-Governance and take it towards M-Governance. The policy would enable citizen to vial of various services online, or at a place near their home, without having to visit Government offices at minimum possible cost .The policy is a step further towards promoting e-Governance in the state .The e-Governance policy objective is to ensure standardized and seamless implantation of e-Governance projects across state policy issued several guidelines about use of UID; use of Marathi language in e-Governance implantation, Utilization of multiple service delivery channels to provide citizens services at their doorsteps various citizens services shall be made available online through the state portal to be developed in line with the National portal and through other channels like CSC (Maha e-seva Kendra) SETU, common Facilities center (OFC) etc. state service Delivery Gateway services building, joint venture, collaboration and partnership with private companies.

Digital services in Maharashtra

The state of Maharashtra is all set to log on to a future of digitally empowered governance system from 2ndOctober 2017 the government of Maharashtra will provide all citizen centric services through digital platforms making a major step towards delivery on the prime Minister's promise of "maximum governance, minimum government"[10] sharing his vision for a digitally empowered state the Maharashtra former Chief Minister Devendra Fadanvis stated " dream of the Maharashtra where the government proactively engages with citizens through social media platforms once all the citizen services on Aapale Sarkar portal are made available on its mobile app. no citizen of my state will have to visit a government office to resolve matters the entire spectrum of government related applications and payment gateways will be available to him on mobile."

The Digital empowerment measure will result in radical transformation in the way the citizens interface with the government it will eliminate human intervention ensuring transparency, accuracy, efficiency and inclusion However that he will continue to work towards function of his paradigm shift "On 2nd October 2017 almost 75% of my task will be accomplished in a year.[11] Time within a year we will be able to integrate all backend activities and then I will be able to claim that the citizens of my state will not have to visit any government office to avail of any citizen service. Maharashtra state is a first state to implement the crime and criminal tracking network system (CCTYS)[12] system in a comprehensive manner launched in September 2015, the Rs 2000 crore e- Governance project connect all police stations digitally.

Especially in Nanded district of the state the public Distribution system (PDS) has been digitalized recently. I helps to control bogus beneficiaries, to decrease malpractices in administration and also various ration shop. Nanded Municipal corporation providing many services through digital way very important thing is that Nanded is the first District in the state to introduce special websites to its tahasil offices and sub divisional offices Nanded is always a pioneer district to provide e-Governance through various project Nanded has made its mark by digitalizing its administration and the services on the occasion of Independence Day, Nanded has launched its application that called

'Aapala Nanded' it gives information about all the developments and scheme to the public.[13]

Concept of E-Governance/Administration

Governance refers to that structures and processes that are designed to ensure to ensure accountability, transparency, responsiveness, rule of law, stability, equity and inclusiveness, empowerment and broad – based participation .

Especially, e-Governance is defined as "the application of ICT to transform the efficiency, effectiveness, transparency and accountability of exchange Information and transaction between government and citizen, between government and business through e-governance, government services will be made available to citizens in a convenient, efficient and transparent manner.

According to World Bank "e-Governance refers to the use of government agencies of Information technologies (such as wide Area Net works, the Internet and mobile Computing) that have the ability to transform relation with citizens, Business, and other arms of government".[14]

UNESCO:-e-Governance as "Governance refers to the exercise of political economic and administrative authority in the management of a Country's affairs, including citizen's articulation of their interest and exercise of their legal rights and obligation. E-Governance may be understood as the performance of this governance via the electronic medium in order to facilitate an efficient, speedy and transparent process of disseminating information to the public and to other agencies while performing government Administration activities.

Meaning of Digital:-(according to oxford dictionary)

Relating to or using signals represented as digits using discrete values of a physical quantity such as voltage or magnet polarization. Compare with analogue involving or relating to the use of computer technology.[15]

Digital Administration

Digital administration is a ensure that Government services are made available to citizens electronically by improved. Online infrastructure and by increasing internet connectivity or by making the country digitally empowered in the field to technology.

Good Governance

Good governance is an approach to government that is committed to creating a system founded in justice and peace that protects individual's human right and civil liberties. According to the united Nation, Good governance is measured by the eight factors of participation, Rules of Law, Transparency, Responsiveness, Consensus oriented, Equity and Inclusiveness, Effectiveness and efficiency, and Accountability.[16]

"SMART Governance is about using technology to facilitate and support better planning and decision making it is about improving democratic processes and transforming the ways that public services are delivered. It included e-Government, the efficiency agenda and mobile working".

Open Government

According to the Obama administration government should be transparent and provide information for its citizens on what it is doing .The administration called for executive department and agencies to use new information technology to put information about their operation and decision online and make it reality available to the public Farmer President of USA Obama on issued a memorandum on Transparency and open government[17].

E-Democracy

E-democracy also known as digital democracy or internet democracy incorporates 21st century information and communication technology to promote democracy. It is form of government in which all adult citizens are presumed to be eligible to participate equally in the proposal, development, and creation of laws.[18]

Importance of Digital Administration for the society

Indian Government has started implementation of Digital Administration state wise project like Maharashtra. Setusuvidha kentra, Aapalesarakar portal, Friends for Kerala government, E-seva for Andhra Pradesh, Bhoomi for Karnataka etc. Todays every state has started implementation of digital administration project, so following are the importance of Digital Administration project.

Building Strong and Effective Information chain

Citizen can take benefits of Digital Administration project for getting effective information effectively and every easily. Information chain can be very much effective using Digital Administration project. Most of the data like statistics, personal records, general Information regarding any city we can find easily by filling application ever the Internet /website, government can also look back that who is interested in which kind of data so they can provide subscribe facilities and can give up to date information to the citizen.

(2) Fast and Convenient service to Citizen

Digital Administration is the way to provide information very fast and effectively to the citizens of the country so the citizen can apply using online application can get information Vise-mail or Web portal developed by the government so he/she can get documents easily in electronic form or hard copy as per the request, so no more waiting in the queue and can apply online. In other way we can take advantage of many other online services using websites or portal and also mobile apps.

(3) Decreased Red Tape and Corruption

Digital Administration an opportunity for improvement in public service delivery and most administrative best practices build upon the process redesign and convergence those Digital Administration facilities. Digital governance leads to a transformation in work processed and service delivery, lowers transaction cost with improvement in transparency and accountability. Digital Administration can help reduce corruption and improve accountability by making budgets so digital governance reduce the delay, fast the procedures and reduce the corruption through transparency.[19]

(4) For the Communities

Using Digital Administration we can integrate each department with each other and can get advantage of the integration. This kind of integration is implemented in the video conferencing websites, E-mail.

Save time and Money

In 21st century many peoples are using the digital services therefore they save their time and money.

References

1. Eapen, K.V. (2018), *Effective grievance redressal Hart of Good governance*, (Yojana journal.) New Delhi, Government of India, p. 07
2. Sari, Yogesh and other, (Feb-2018) *New India 2022.* Yojana journal, New Delhi, government of India. p. 20
3. Tom Butler, Joseph feller, (2005) *Promoting knowledge sharing in government and non government organization.* Annual Conference, 29 June 2005 Florence lately. p. 28.
4. Https//it mission: kerala gov. in/achievement
5. https//itmission:kerala.gov.in/achievement
6. https//deity.gov.in/content/national e-governance palm.
7. Dua, Seema (2016) *Digital India opportunities & challenges* two days international conference, dev. Samaj college for women, ferozepur, Punjab. p. 217.
8. Omkar ray, (2017) *Digital India program*, yojana (marathi) May 2017, New Delhi, government of India, p. 10.
9. https:Maharashtra.gov.in/*e-governance policy*/pdf
10. https://econmictimes/dated03nov2017Online news paper.
11. https://Ibid. p. 04
12. ibid. p. 04
13. https://nanded-gov.in/apps/Aaple nanded.
14. https://worldbank.org/extintormation and communication and technologies/ p. 01
15. Oxford online Dictionary.
16. https://Creativelearimg.org./blog./2016/11/08/what is-good-governance/
17. Christopher, G., jones & Bartleft (2012), *Public administration and information technology.* Canada, p. 34.
18. https://en.m.wikipedia.org/wikile-democracy.
19. hhttps://nceg.gov.in/naeg201

Chapter - 2

History and Development of Digital Administration

Introduction

Digital Administration refers to the application of the internet and other information technology (IT) to provide governmental information and services electronically it offers the potential of increased convenience to the public by making such services available 24 hours a day a week, coupled with the advantages of improved accuracy and also reduced cost to the government, deriving from its requiring little or no direct interaction with a government employee.[1]

The interaction between a citizen and a government agency takes place in a government office with emerging information and communication technologies it is possible to locate service centres closed to citizens.

Digital Governance/Administration, its impacts on society and its practical models time what the role model information technologies in achieving goals under Digital Governance is, whether Digital Governance is a revolutionary instrument for transformation the way the government around the world govern their citizens and what those theoretical models of Digital Governance are that my help government to ensure delivery of services and facilities to the citizens at their door step.

The U.S federal government is not alone in realizing the potential benefits of e-government. E-government services are also offered by all the state many municipalities and indeed by the government of most of the world's development countries. A number of efforts by varied groups, including the united Nations (UN) and the American society for public administration (ASPA), researchers at brown university, and various consultancies have begun to compare e-government offerings internationally, Typically, these groups have found that the quality of the government offerings of the U.S federal government is among the best world-wide, although public adoption of such services has been found to be higher in some other countries.[2] for example, Accenture's January 2005 survey of people in the united states found that over 55% had made at least some use of e-government; the same survey found that almost 70 % of those surveyed used the internet at least once a month. Accenture also found that reported use of e-government was higher in Australia, Canada, and Singapore, Norway, Denmark, Sweden and Finland with higher percentages of people using.[3]

In the 21st Century the priorities of the governments changed to work towards economic competitiveness provide digital service to citizen, encourage e-communities and digital democracy while continuing to upgrade education and equip citizen's for the 'Knowledge Century' so, there was a need to take stroke and re-invent Government by Re-thinking the Goals of Government; Re-assessing the organisation and culture; Re-engineering the business processes and finally Implementing New government not only that government emphasized on 24/7 working, flexi-Time for employee flatter organisational hierarchies clear benchmarking of performance and higher accountability, and lower quantity but higher quality of governance as the norm in short a vision directed citizens focused plat, empowered, global networked and electronic government is emerging.

Digital Administration Initiatives in world

Digital reform followed through to Today's Estonia first Digitalized country in the world so the detail information of the country Estonia.

Estonia refers to a movement by the government of Estonia to facilitate citizen interaction with the state through the use of electronic solutions e-services created under this initiative include i-voting, e-Tax board, e-Business, e-Banking, e-ticket, e-school, university via internet, the governance Academy as well as the release of several mobile application.[4]

Estonia:-In 1991, Estonia restored its independence as a sovereign nation, defeating the soviet occupation prior to this, there was little in the way of technology. under half or its population had a phone line following independence, the first prime minister Mart Laar helped push the country through a period of modernization establishing the foundation needed to bring the country into the digital age.

The present, Early during the reform Estonia refused on offer from Finland to give it its old analogue telephone exchange for free, electing instead to build its own digital phone system .An initiative to provide school with computers succeed with internet access by 1998 in 2000, the government declared internet access to be human right, causing its spread into rural areas.[5]

E-Residency:-In late 2014, Estonia became the first country to offers electronic residency to people from outside the country, a step that the Estonia government terms as "moving towards in idea of a country without borders." Under this program on-residents can apply to have a smart ID card issued to them by the state providing the same access to Estonia's various electronic services that a physical resident would be given.

Digital 5:- The first event of D5was held in Landon on 9& 10 December 2014 with delegate from five founding nations attending, as well as the united states, who were there as observers, the event was hosted by the UK'S cabinet office ministers Francis Maude. The founding members of the Digital 5 group are1**.** Estonia 2.Israel 3. New Zealand 4. South Korea 5.United Kingdom[6]

Since February 2018 Canada, Uruguay include the Digital 7 group this summit theme had three themes 1. Teaching children to code 2. Open markets 3. Connectivity

Digital signature in Estonia

Electronic signature allows users to electronically perform the actions for which they previously had to give a signature on paper .Estonia's digital signature system is the foundation for some of its most popular e-services including registering company.

Top Digital Countries[6]

The UK government is one of the award digitally advanced in

the world. We have developed the award winning and internationally renowned Government UK and have opened its code, which has been reused by governments around the world. The government Digital service has led the digital transformation of government and is model that is being copies internationally

Table: E-Government development and E Participation index

Developmetn Index			E-Participation Index		
Sr. No.	**Country**	**Index**	**Sr. No**	**Country**	**Index**
1.	Denmark	0.9150	1.	Republic of dorea	1.0000
2.	Australia	0.9053	2.	Denmark	1.0000
3.	Republic of korea	0.9010	3.	Finland	1.0000
4.	United kingdom	0.8999	4.	Netherland	0.9888
5.	Sweden	0.8882	5.	Japan	0.9831
6.	Finland	0.8815	6.	New Zealand	0.9831
7.	Singzpore	0.8812	7.	Australia	0.9831
8.	New Zealand	0.8806	8.	Spain	0.9831
9.	France	0.8790	9.	United kingdom	0.9831
10.	Japan	0.8783	10.	USA	0.9831

Source:- United nation e-governance survy report 2018[7].

The unranking are based on three main criteria that allow people to benefit from online services and information adequacy of telecommunication infrastructure, the ability of human resources to promote and use ICT and the availability of online services and content.

Many countries in the world have taken notice of these development and are utilizing the technologies to further their national vision in this regard Australia has formulated their vision to be world leader in government administration and in the cost effective provision of affordable, equitable and accessible Australian government information services

Canada: - has adopted a vision of "Government services that are affordable, accessible and responsive." Their initiative connecting Canadians has put in place the necessary strategies and initiative, security standards based secure architecture for all department etc.

Singapore: - has a vision to transform Singapore into an intelligent Island, where the use of information technology is pervasive in every aspect of its society at work, home and play. Their e governance initiatives started way back in 198 and today the Singapore one network has provided high bandwidth to 99 per cent of the citizens. The e citizen centre portal to provide public services started as a pilot and has expended into public service online today over 130 services are online.

United kingdom:- is best place world for e governance towards this UK has developed a government portal with single point access to government and various services. Anew office of e-envoy with a budget of GBP 2 billion and 200 employees has been established to oversee the process and in answerable directly to the prime minister. They have put all services online expect few. which are in the process.

China:-Central and local government have integrated information with their economic and social development plan and made it a strategic move towards prosperity they delivered 80 per cent administrative service via the internet and are addressing issues of necessary infrastructure creating a domestic information industry and bridging the "digital drive" between their less developed and more developed regions in the country[8].

Mexico:-Mexico has an area of 2 million square kilometres with a nine thousand kilometres coastline and a climate chat varies from tropical to desert.

By the early 1300 AB the Aztec established roots on an island in lake Mexico, site of present day Mexico city in 1521 the Spanish explorer Herman Cortez captured and razed the Aztec city building a Spanish city in its place in 1821. Mexican revolutionaries captured Mexico City and broke all ties with the Spanish crown. The city was occupied by the United States in 1847 during the Mexican war and by France for four years starting in 1862.

Today Mexico has a GDP of 448 billion with 4% growth in 1999. It has 23 internet hosts for every 10,000 population, 112 Telephones mainlines per 1000 population and 44 pcs per 1000 population. The Mexican Gov. has adopted on ambitious plan to reduce the digital device that exists in country though the development of national system called e Mexico that will allow the greatest possible part of the population to have access to Its (http://www.e-Mexico.gob.MX) the purpose of this initiative in to enable citizens to communicate themselves, with their government and with the rest of the world.

Best Digital Governance Models

Model of Digital governance are still evolving countries and continuously improvising to fully bind the potential of knowledge networks. A few generic models however have shaped up which are finding greater recognition and are being replicated. These models are based on the internet characteristics of ICT which are enabling equal access to information to anyone who is a part of the digital network and DE concentration of information across the entire digital network. The resulting benefits can be less corruption, increased transparency, greater suitability, revenue growth, and/ or cost reduction.[9]

There are five models of Digital Governance as given by pro. Dr.Arie Halachimi which can be used as a guide in designing Digital governance initiative depending on local situation and governance activities that are expected to be delivered

1. Broadcasting model

In this as name implies information is broadcast to wider public domain through use of ICT and convergent media. This models strength is its focus on spreading information to wider mass and through this citizen will be able to judge functioning of existing government mechanism and able to talk informed decision. This empowers them and they are in a better position to exercise their rights and responsibilities.

Projects:-

1. India:- Directory of official websites of Government of India:- http://goidirectory.nic.in
2. Brazil:- Brazil's official national e-government website: http// www.brazil.gov.br
3. South Africa:- Chapter 2 Network: http:/www.advocacy.org.
4. Global:- Earth Negotiation Bulletin http://www.isd.ca/voltoc.html

2 Critical –Flow Model

The Model is based on channelling information of critical value to a targeted audience or dissemination it in the wider public domain through the use of ICT and convergent media. The models requires foresight to understand the significance of a particular information set and using it strategically it may also involve locating users to whom the availability of a particular information set would make a critical difference in initiating good governance. The strength of critical flow model is the inherent characteristic of ICT that makes the notion of distance and time redundant .This reduces the case of exploitative governance possible earlier due to time day between availability of information to different users.

Projects:-

1. India- central vigilance committee (India) http://cvc.nic.in the website provides free access information to citizens about government officials who have been indicted on judicial charges relating to corruption and have been advised penalty.
2. Bangladesh:- Human right portal :http/www.banglaright.net

The Bangladesh Human rights Network actively promotes human right and supports women children; and marginalized communities in resisting social oppression

Global:- Transparency international's corruption

News:-http://www.transparency.org/press.moni,html

Atrial service run by Transparency international called the Daily corruption News which reports on corruption from around the world.

3. Comparative Analysis Model

The comparative analysis model is based on exploring information available in the public or private domain and comparing it with the known information sets to drive strategic learning and arguments. The model continuously assimilate new knowledge products and use them as a benchmark to evaluate, influence or advocate change in current governance policies and action the comparison could be made over a time scale to get a snapshot of the two different situation to understand the effectiveness of an invention. The strength of this model lies in the boundless capacity of ICT to store information in a retrievable manner and transmit it almost instantaneously across all geographical and hierarchical barriers.

Projects:-

1. **India:-**Comparative Learning from Disasters after the devastating earthquake in Kutch in 2001 learning on disaster management was down by comparing it with the high intensity earthquake that shook Latur in India in 1993. The extensive information available on internet on both these earthquake open up vast scope of comparison by all segments of the society .An example of disaster comparison made by an officers of the Indian Administrative service (IAS) digital gov/Latur Gujarat.htm.

2. **Philipplnes:-** vote,ph:http/www.vote.ph

   Global:- Human Development in dictators

   http//www.undp.org/hdro/indicators

4. Mobilisation and Lobbying Model

This Model is on of the most frequently used. Digital Governance model and has often come to the aid of the global civil society to impact on global decision making processes. This model is based on planned defected strategic flow of information complement to build strong virtual allies to complement action in real world it takes up a pro-active approach of forming virtual communities which share similar values and concerns pro noting active sharing of information within and between these communities, and linking them with real life groups/activities for concerted action. The model creates synergize between real world process and concerns expressed by virtual communities.

Projects:-

Global:- Independent media centre http//www.indymedia.org/

The centre was established by various independent and alternative media organisations to grassroots coverage of WTO settle in 1999.

Greenpeace cyber-activist community:-

http://Cyber centre.greenpeace.org//t/s

India:-Panchayats: - http//www.panchyats.org

5. Interactive service Model

The interactive service model is a consolidation of the earlier model and open up avenues for direct participation of individuals in m the government process. Fundamentally, ICT have the potential to bring in every individual in a digital network and enable two-way/ interactive flow of information amongst them. The potential of ICT for the governance is a fully leveraged in this model and leads to greater participation, efficiency and transparency in functioning of the government as well as savings in time and cost relating to decision making.

Projects:-

Philippine:-Philippine custom reform

http://www.worldbank.org/publicsector/egov/

India:-Gyandoot:http://www.gyandoot.net/

Gyandoot is an internet in Ohar district of Madhya Pradesh connecting rural cyber cafes catering to everyday needs of the masses. The site offers several interactive governance related services to the local people such as providing copies of land –maps online registration of application and public grievance redressed it is a step towards tele centre based Digital governance models.

The digital governance model bring about a transformation in the exciting from of governance as they change the nature of citizen-governance relationship and bring in new agents and mechanisms to influence the governance processes. The models foster democratic control ever the governments economics, social and welfare policies by citizens and civil society organisations a key process requirement for good and responsive governance it ensure that the voices of people are more likely to be reflected in decision making processes.

Digital Administration Initiatives in India

The technology as well as e-governance initiatives have come a long way since them. Recognizing the increasing importance of electronics, the Government of India established the Department of electronics in 1970.[10] The subsequent establishment of the National Informatics centre (NIC) in 1997 was the first major step towards e-Governance in India as it brought information and its communication in focus. Through, the late 1980[s] a signification number of govt. officials used computers, but their application were restricted to world processing only in 1987, with launch of the national satellite based computer network (NIC NET), the governance agenda in India gained momentum. NIC NET was extended via the state capitals tom all district headquarters by 1990.

India Portal –Mission Mode project (MMP)

Indian portal project has been identified as one of the Mission Mode project in the integrated service under the National e-Governance plan (NeGP) of Government of India. The portal is envisaged to provide a single window access to the information and service of the Indian Government for the citizens corporate organisations both in state and non-state sectors the Government itself media and the world at large.

The first version of the portal is operational now and was launched by Hon'ble Union Minister for communications and IT, Tritu Dayanidhi Maran in a public function on 10th November 2005[11] the portal address is http://India.gov.in/Hon'ble Deputy chairman planning commission shri. Montek Singh Ahluwalia presided over the function.

Initiative on National e-Governance service Delivery Gateway (NSDG)

The National e-Governance service Delivery Gateway is one of the 31 mission mode project under the National plan of GOI [12]aims to make all Government services accessible to the common man is his locality, through common service delivery outlets and ensure efficiency, transparency and reliability of such services at affordable costs to realize the basic needs to co-operate, collaborate & integrate information across different Department in the centre, state, and Local Government systems characterized by islands of legacy systems using heterogeneous platforms and technologies and spread across diverse geographical Locations in varying state of automation, make this task very challenging, the task by acting as standards- based messaging switch and providing seamless interoperability and exchange of data across.

State Data Centre (SDC)

State Data centre has been identified as one of the important element of the core infrastructure for supporting e-Governance plan

(NEGP) under NeGP it is proposed to create state Data centres for the state to consolidate services, applications and infrastructure to provide efficient. Electronic delivery of G2G, G2C, & G2B services. These services can be rendered by the state through common delivery platform seamlessly supported by core connectivity infrastructure such as state wide area Network (Swan) and common service centre (CSC)connectivity extended up to village level.

SDC scheme has been approved by Government with an outlay of 1623.20crores over a period of 5 year.[13]

State Wide Area Network (SWAN)

The Government had approved the scheme for establishing state wide Area Network (SWAN) across the country in March,2005 at a total outlay of Rs.3,334 Crore to be expended by the Department under Grant-in-Aid of Rs 2,005 crore over a period of five years. Under this scheme technical and financial assistance are being provided to the state/ UTS for establishing SWANS to connect all state/UT Headquarters up to the block level via District/sub-Divisional Headquarters in a vertical hierarchical structure with a minimum capacity of 2Mbps per link. Each of the state/UT can enhance the band width up to 34 Mbps between SHQ and DHQ and up to 8mbph between SHQ and BHQ depending upon the utilization.

Common services centres (under NeGP)

CSC is strategic corner stone of the National e-Governance plan (NeGP) approved by the Government in may 2006 as part of commitment in the National common minimum programme to introduce e-governance on a massive scale.

The CSCs would provide high quality and cost effective video, voice and data Content and services, in the areas of e-Governance., education, health, Telemedicine, entertainment as well as other private services. A highlight of the CSC that it will offer web-enable e-governance services in rural areas, including application forms, certificates and Utility payment such as electricity, Telephone and water bills in addition tom the Universe of G2C .

Common Services Centres (Under Digital India programme)

CSC means common services centres schemes is one the mission mode projects under the Digital India programme.

CSC are the access points for delivery essential public utility services, social welfare schemes health care, Financial, education & agriculture services apart prom host of B2c services to citizens in rural and remote areas of the country it is a plan India network catering to regional, geographic, linguistic and cultural diversity of the country thus enabling the Governments mandate of a socially, Financially and digitally inclusive society.

The CSC projects which forms a strategic component of the National e-Governance plan was approved in September 2006 it is also one of the approved projects under the integrated Mission Mode Projects under the Integrated mission mode projects of the National e-Governance plan. The implementation of the CSC would be done in a public-private partnership model whereby the total project cost of Rs.57.42 billion, over 4 years, would be shared between Government (30%equal to Rs. 16.49 billion) and private Finances (70 % equal to Rs.40.93 billion)[14] The split between central and state government would be Rs. 8.56 billion and Rs.7.93 billion respectively. As of 31st Jan 2011, 88,689 CSC have been rolled out in 11 state is expected that roll out of 100,000 CSC would be completed by March 2011.

CSC 2.0 scheme, the Government launched the CSC 2.0 Scheme in 2015 to expand the outreach of CSCS to all Grampanchyats cross the country under CSC 2.0 scheme, at least one CSC will be set up in each of the 2.5 Lakhs GPs across the country by 2019. CSC functioning under the existing scheme will also be strengthened and integrated with additional 1.5 Lakhs CSCS across the country CSC 2.0 scheme would consolidate service delivery through a universal Technology platform, thereby making e-services, particularly G2c service accessible to citizens any where in the country. CSC centre was 83,000 Today CSC centre 3 Lakhs is a working Honourable prime Minister Shri. Narendra Modi appreciated the efforts of 3 Lakh common services centres [15]across India in Digital Empowerment of people during inauguration of centre for the 4th Industrial Revolution here in New Delhi on 11th October 2018. He said that 3 Lakhs CSCs across the country are playing vital role in Digital Empowerment in rural India.

Digital India Programme

Government of India across the highest priority to the Digital India

Programme that is an Umbrella programme for transforming India into a digitally empowered society and knowledge economy, e-kranti is an integral part of the Digital India Programme with the vision of "Transforming e-Governance for Transforming Governance." The mission of e-Krantis "To ensure a Government wide transformation by delivery all Government services electrically the citizens through integrated and interoperable efficiency, Transparency and reliability of such services at affordable costs." The Union cabinet in its meeting held on 25.03.2015 has approved the approach and key components of e-kranti that includes, inter alia, the vision, mission, key principals of e-kranti, Approach and Methodology, programme Management structure and Implementation strategy including 44 Mission Mode projects and core ICT Infrastructure. The Digital India programme and specially its pillar 4and pillar 5namely e-Governance Reforming Government through Technology and e-kranti electronic Delivery of services respectively are directly linked with e-kranti and the implementation of e-kranti is critical for the success of e-Governance, easy governance and good governance in the country.

Digital India is a campaign launched by the Government of India to ensure the Governments services are mode available to citizens electronically by improved online infrastructure and by increasing internet connectivity or by making the country digitally empowered in the field of technology[16]The initiative includes plans to connect rural areas with high-speed internet networks. Digital India consists of three core components.

1. Development of square and stable digital infrastructure
2. Delivering government services digitally and
3. Universal digital literacy

Digital India was launched by the prime Minister of India Narendra Modi on 1st July 2015 with on Objective of connecting rural areas with high speed internet networks and improving digital literacy. The vision of digital India programme is inclusive growth in areas of ele3ctronic services, products, manufacturing and job opportunities etc., and it is centred on three Key areas-Digital Infrastructure as activity to every citizen, Governance and services on Demand and Digital Empowerment of citizens.

The Government of India enquiry Bharat Broadband Network Limited (BBNL) which executes the Bharat Net project is the custodian of Digital India project Bharat Net will connect all the 625,000 villages of India by December 2018.

The vision of Digital India is grand it is a huge step towards building a truly empowered nation if successful, it transform citizen access to multimedia information content and services. However the goal is still far away since most of the nine pillars of digital India mission are facing serious challenges in implementation.

M-Governance

M-governance is a sub-domain of e-governance it ensures that electronic services are available to people via mobile phone. These services bypass the need for traditional physical networks for communication and collaboration mobile services are also cheaper as well as accessible in most of the rural areas in India.

Increasing the mobile phone accessibility, adaptability and with the millions of subscription base, government are promoting and using the mobile phone in delivery the e-governance in the last few years, government have seen mobile phone can empower citizens and affect the way citizens interact with each other and with society at large, Mobile in strengthening democracy through better citizen -governance interaction thus influencing the political decision making process and making government accountable for their activities.

Government of India aims to utilize the massive reach of mobile phones and harness the potential of mobile application to enable easy and round – the clock access to public services, especially in the rural application development ecosystem for m-Governance in the country. The Government of India is implementing the "Digital India." Programme with a vision to transform India into a digitally empowered society and knowledge economy under the Digital India programme, e-kranti on rises provisioning of various e-governance services in the country. The focus of the e-rant programme is to transform the e-Governance services by expanding the Portfolio of Mission Mode projects (MMPs) in e-Governance under various Government Departments undertaking Government process reengineering work flow automation, introducing latest technologies such as cloud and mobile platform and focus on integration of services.

The ministry of Electronics and information Technology developed and notified the framework for mobile. Governance in February 2012 the M-governance framework of Government of India aims to utilize the massive reach of mobile applications to enable easy and round. The clock access to public services, especially in the rural areas. The framework aims to create unique infrastructure as well as application development ecosystem for m-governance in the country.

Towards Smart Governance

In the 21st century, the democratic states have become a synonym of a welfare state. The democratic government acts as a services provider. The machinery to reach to its citizen and provide necessary services in a efficient and equitable manner.

'**SMART**' captures the important attributes of Good Governance i.e. simple, Moral, Accountable, Responsive and Transparent government. It is necessary to discuss these five attributes to understand them and to know that can be achieved from these elements with electronic intervention. "Simple" citizen expects a user friendly government with simplicity of Laws, rules, regulations and processes, procedures formulated by the government. The multiplicity of laws and their complex procedures with the requirement of many proofs drive citizens to middle men, resulting in delay and corrupt practices to avoid these situations with the help of e-governance; government is implementing "single window" one stop services through CSC to facilitate common citizen under the Digital India programme.

'**Moral**' the "Moral" in SMART" governance denotes emergence of new system of governance based on Moral values. The "cleaning up process is very slow but it is very essential for the survival of values cherished by Good Governance some of the processes like systematic changes in electoral reforms downsizing of government, enhancing literacy, increasing awareness and participation can take a longer duration to show its effects. However, such programmes should not be overlooked.

'**Accountability**' it is the soul of a democratic government and the very corner stone of public Administration.

'**Responsiveness**'- It refers to the needs of common man. A responsive Administration shows urgency in responding to different problems faced by the common man charter developed in 1990in the UK[17] can be used to improve the responsiveness of the government. Citizens charter is a set of assurances given by the government agency on the quality of service and time limit for delivery.

'Transparency' Transparency brings some of the essential virtues in to public life. Such as equality, level playing field and the rule of law. These virtues confer social benefits to the people with no discretion and no scope of corruption. 'Transparency' arises out of the citizen's Right to Information, right to know why certain decision was taken. The deployment of ICT can quickly disseminate information through the use of web sites or portals which can be used to form decisions, opinions. Government of India through decentralization of power and citizens empowerment, trying for effective citizen participation at all levels in program and civic service reforms.

The five principles of SMART governance are relevant to the working of public sector. If e-governance systems are designed and built to enhance these principles in practice they can provide multiple benefits to its users.

Digital Administration Initiatives in Maharashtra

Maharashtra has been a pioneer in the adoption of technology that improves transparency and accountability of the government the efforts of the state have been focused on coupling Technology initiatives with overall Administration, aiming to take the government to the citizens' doorsteps and usher in a digitally inclusive society. Maharashtra is the first state to have a dedicated e-governance policy which was drafted by a 10-member e-governance committee under the chairmanship of Dr. Vijay Batkar and approved by the cabinet. The policy was published on September 23,2011 and the implementation plan issued on April 10, 2012.[18] The state government has adopted e-governance and m-governance to reach out to citizens in more effective manners and the conventional functioning processes are being revamped through exhaustive Business process Reengineering and electronic service delivery. The state government has focused on the following vital points:-

1. Creation of Capacity-building infrastructure

This includes opening of It academics in Pune, Aurangabad and

Nagpur an it and e-governance Training Room in Mantralaya, and revamp of It infrastructure of 152 state training institutes.

2. Policy level interventions

The Maharashtra government has taken the following policy-level interventions.

1. Maharashtra information Technology virtual Cadre.
2. Students internships with government of Maharashtra which will help them acquire a theoretical level of understanding-governance.
3. MOU (Memorandum of understanding) between DIT (Directorate of Information Technology), Government of Maharashtra and YASHADA (Yeshwantrao Chavhan Academy of Development Administration) to promote it training of government officials.

3. Training workshops and leaderships

Under this category, Government of Maharashtra conducts regular training programmes, workshops and leadership summits for its officers and employees on various aspects of e-governance. These Training and workshops are also attended by other stakeholders like consultants, software programmers working with the state government, media personnel etc. These have also witnessed participation from other state governments.

Another important initiative of the Maharashtra Government is the launch of e-governance Training and certification, the first and only free online certification, course in e-governance in India[19] managed by the Directorate of information Technology (DIT), Government of Maharashtra, based on the concept of MOOC. This certification has been made mandatory for all staff members in mandatory for all staff-members in DIT, as well as consultants and software developers working in the e-governance space in Maharashtra.

However, the number of people enrolling for certification and the number of candidates passing the exam shows a worrisome picture the following chart from the 'state of e-Governance in Maharashtra 2014'report shows the number of batches that enrolled in the year 2014 and the candidates that passed certification against it.

The e-Governance status Report 2014 its salient Features

The e-governance status Report 2014 of Maharashtra also focuses on aspects of inclusion through citizen centricity and Ease of use its salient Features.

(i) No Affidavits:-

To make services available to citizens standardised and hassle-free manner, the Directorate of Information Technology has come up with a GR that would replace the filing an affidavit along with the application with a self-Declaration, A Government Resolution to this effect was issued on August 14 2013.[20]

(ii) Format Standardization:-

Sixteen revenue services including income certificates Residence certificates, age, Nationality and Domicile certificates, solvency certificates, senior citizen, Birth, Death certificates etc., have been standardized across all districts in Maharashtra. These are extremely important services especially for the poor and it is an important step towards ensuring better service delivery for citizens.

(iii) Rate Standardization:-

Rates of Government to Citizen Services provided through different delivery mechanisms like common services centres, Sangrams, Setu; Mahaonline etc. have been standardized across Maharashtra. The same fee shall be charged to citizens irrespective of mode of delivery. However, this may not be ideal as the socially backward and require concessional rates and in some instance free access to these services.

(iv) Localisation:-

Marathi has been made the First and mandatory language in all e-governance services across the state of Maharashtra. This is an important step towards ensuring inclusion in e-governance.

(v) E-Scholarships for Tribal, SC, and Minorities:-

Tribal Development Department, Minorities Development Department and Social Justice and special Assistance Department, provide various scholarships to students from socially backward and economically weaker Families in the state. Initially, the scholarships were disbursed manually; but now all of these departments have automated the process and implemented e-scholarship system enables online application, automated approval, Transparent verification and timely disbursement of scholarship under this new system the scholarships is credited directly into the accounts of students; and they also receive a confirmation SMS alert from the system. The solution user interface is available in English and Marathi.

(vi) Online Disability Certificates

Doctors can issue five Types of disability certificates – viz, Visual, Hearing, Physical, Mental illness and mental Retardation using the software for Assessment of Disability, Maharashtra (SADM) Doctors only need to enter the4 assessment values and the disability percentage is calculated automatically by the software. These certificated are directly linked with the UID.

(vii) e-Validity for Caste certificates and Minority status Certificates:-

This application enables online application, verification, approval/rejection and finally online delivery of caste certificates and Minority status certificates to citizens. Throughout the process, updates to citizens on the status of their application are sent regularly.

It is clear that after seeing the history and development of Digital Administration from globally to the state level, in the cases of the First case, Estonia country is the First known as the Digital Country. Kerala is recognized as the state of digital India in the Country, and it has also been studied the history and development of Digital governance in India, including Governance etc. and finally the study of history and development of Digital Administration of Maharashtra. After this study national, state-level projects models and status of Digital Administration will be studied in the next chapter.

References

1. National Research Council (2007) *Social security Administration electronic service provision A strategic Assessment*, p. 48.
2. http://nap. edu/read/11 920/chapter/11/# p. 20013.
3. http://www.accenture.com/xdoc/10c/june 20, 2007.
4. E-Estonia. Estonia. edu. Estonia. Foreign Ministry and Enterprise Estonia. Retrieved February 2, 2015.
5. Heller, Nathom (2017) "Estonia, The Digital Republic" The New york, p. 23.
6. D5 Landon 2014:- loading digital government Gov. UK. UK. Government. 2014 (online-eBook)
7. http://google weblight.com/i2u= http://public Administration un.org/e gov kb/en.us/ Report un.e-Gov.survy2018
8. B Shrinivas Raj(2008) e-Governance Technique New century publications New Delhi; p. 45.
9. http://www.drishtilas.com/UPSC-exam-gs-resources E-Governance m
10. http://www.insightsonindia.com
11. http://india.gov.in / MPPS
12. http://meity.gov,in /division/national-e-governance plan
13. http://meity.gov.in/content/state -data-centre
14. http://nig.org/Knoeledgecentre-docs/A036604
15. CSC monthly magazine October 2018, English
16. Prakash Amit "Digital India needs to golocal" The Hindu. Retried, 26-02-2017. p. 04.
17. http://nesotencil:com/Smart-governance-inindia
18. Maharashtra state e-Government Report, 2014.
19. http://digitalequality.in/history-of-governance in Maharashtra
20. Maharashtra state e-Governance Report, 2014.

Chapter - 3

Mechanism of Digital Administration and Digital Kranti

Introduction

In the previous chapter the history of Digital Administration has been studied then in the present chapter see the mechanism of Digital Administration and the Digital kranti, Today, services in all divisions are being digitalized in the service of the public through the government of India, through the Digital India programme all the services are from the parliament level to Grampanchyat. In this chapter information about what is the digital Administrative machinery of the National level and state of Maharashtra level.

Digitalization started very early in the year. However, the changes due to its low speed were not noticed, initially digital work was done keeping records managing the office, processing information etc., However, research done in the digital revolution since the last few year has created new opportunities. That is why, it is necessary to re-develop the development. Internet, artificial, intelligence, (AI) robotics engineering block chain technology, and other technologies have started social and economic revolution. The development of this technology has given the Indian economy a big boost. This new technique is changing the face of the Indian economy.

E-Kranti Framework

E-governance in India has steadily evolved from computerization of Government Departments to initiatives that encapsulate the finer points of Governance such as citizen centricity, services orientation and transparency.

The National e-Governance plan

The National e-governance plan was conceptualized to focus on e-governance initiatives at the national level with an aim to "make all Government services accessible to the common man in his locality, through common service delivery outlets and ensure efficiency, transparency and reliability of such services affordable cost to realise the basic need of the common man" The Government initially approved the Nation e-Governance plan, comprising of 27 Mission Mode project and 8 components, on May 18, 2006.4 more mission mode projects namely Education, Health, post and public Distribution. Systems were added to NeGp portfolio in 29 July 2011.

Subsequently to the conceptualization of National e-Governance plan 2.0 (NeGp), the 10 MMS. namely e- Sansad, e-vidhan, Financial Inclusion, Road and Highways Information system (RAHI), Agriculture 2.0, National Geographical Information system, Rural Development and common IT Roadmap for para military force are accorded in principle approval by the Apex committee on NeGp headed by cabinet secretary on 18th March, 2014, e-Bhasha, Urban Governance and National Mission on education through ICT are proposed as new MMPS under integrated services category.[1]

Considering the critical need for transforming e-Governance and promote mobile Governance and Good Governance in the country, the approach and key components of e-Kranti have been approved by the union cabinet on 25.03.2015 with the vision of "Transforming e-Governance for transforming governance". On the basis of this entire mission mode project. The central, state Government are providing digital services from all these projects, Our India is becoming Digital, hence, the need of Digital India programme for effective governance is very important today. For the purpose of implementing this effective administration, the project that serves the central and state government in India's projects, the work of serving the people of all India is going on.

Common service Centres (CSC)

The common services centres project, which Component of the

National e-Governance plan was approved in September 2006.[2] It is also one of the approved projects under the integrated Mission mode projects of the National e-governance plan. The implementation of the common service centres would be done in a public –private partnership project(PPP).

In India the work of providing various services in village done Through CSC Ministry of Electronic it (Meity) Government of India in which work is being taken to bring the entrepreneurs ahead and social, financial, Educational, b2c, G2c, services are being provided. Common service centre, special purpose vehicle (CSCSPV) is set up by the companies Act 1956 and by the Ministry of Electronic Information and technology, Government of India.

Today total number of common services centres (csc) in India since 2014, 389,000 has been completed by November 2019.[3]

Current CSC 2.0 modal

Currently csc 2.0 modal is completely based on the services delivery/ transaction oriented reliant entrepreneurship modal, in which the hardware from the Indian government to village –level entrepreneurs and there is no viability gap between structural financing is it was arranged that the applicant should be excited enough for csc centre premiership so that he becomes the operator of social change and fulfils his commitments with commitment. The enthusiastic village level entrepreneurs are adopting this entrepreneurial model, in which village –level entrepreneurs have to manage capital Expenditure and operational Expenditures for the establishment and operation of general services centres.

Under the csc 2.0 scheme are Different service portals at the state/UT level are being integrated in services. In this way e-services especially G2c services, have been made accessible from any were in the country. This will expand the portfolio of services so that they can be accessed equally from each csc. In this way, the stability of the general service centres in rural areas will increase in order to upgrade the daily operations of general services enters and information about these services, village level enterprise are being assisted through training on the enterprise development programme to increase sustainability of village level entrepreneurs, csc 2.0 has recommended that the revenue share between the village level entrepreneurs and other stakeholders is in the ratio of 80.20

In order to ensure standardization in all the states/UTs "National Banding of states/UTs has been started. Each csc has been given a unique identification number and its G is mapping .This provides a Transparent and Accountable monitoring Framework for the e-services being distributed through general service centres. It has happened and the government has helped in solving the gaps in the establishment of a self-sustaining csc network in all the states/UTs.

Women's Participation in system of CSC

Women's participation in the system of common service centres it encourages other women to come forward and established a normal service enters. Individual governments be doing to encourage the women members of self-help groups that gram level entrepreneurs. As a result, 32,361 women entrepreneurs have set up csc[4]

Objectives of CSC 2.0 Model

- Non-discrimination access to e-services for rural citizens by creating csc for entire citizens, using the basic structure already made in reference to other mission mode projects.
- Up to 2.5 lakhs for Grampanchyant level, expansion of voluntary csc network, in each Grampanchyant at least one csc, more than one priority.
- Enabling District e-Governance society for implementation of District Administration.
- Creating strengthening organizational framework for rollout and project, thereby handholding VLES through state management and district administrative machinery and local help desk support.
- Integration and integration of online services into a signal technology platform, this is service delivery to the responsible, transparent, efficient, and searchable service delivery of cscs with technology-based relationship among all stakeholders.
- Provide a centralized technology forum for the delivery of various servicesto the citizens through a transparent way.

- VLES increased stability by encouraging Maximum commissions and VLES obtained by e-services delivery.

Participating in csc scheme & eligibility

1. Must be young in the village that is more than 18 year old.
2. He should be 10th standard exam from recognized board.
3. In order to read and write local language the applicant should be sharp 4. and have basic Knowledge of English.
5. Early Knowledge will be useful in basis computer skills.
6. Must be a valid Adhar number.

Essential infrastructure for csc

1. Pcs with operating system of windows xp-sp2 or above.

   Minimum 120 GB hard disk drive
2. Minimum 512 MB RAM
3. CD/DVD drive
4. Ups with 4 hour battery back-up/portable generator set
5. Printers/colour printers and scanners
6. Web camera/digital camera
7. For internet browsing and data uploading at least 128 kbps speed internet connection.
8. Biometric/IRIS authentication scanner for banking services.

CSC's services

The CSCs services will provided high quality and cost effective video, Voice and data content services, in the context of e-governance, education, health, telemedicine, entertainment and other private services. One highlight of the csc is that they will of for applications forms certificates and utility payments like web enable e-governance services in rural area such as electricity, Telephone and water bills in addition to the universe of G2c service a wide variety of content and services are offered.

Available Digital services on common services centres

In addition to the G2C, B2C services feast csc is the entry point for public utility services, social welfare schemes, healthcare, financial, schemes, delivery to rural and rural people. It is a an all India network providing regional, geographic, linguistic, and cultural diversity across the country, enabling government order of social, economic and digital inclusive society. The following services are provided by the csc network.

Government services for the citizens (G2c)

An important order of the csc schemes is to provide civilian services by the government.(G2c) A part from state-specific services, central Government of Various Ministries and Department have been integrated to distribute the services to rural and remote areas of the country to the csc network.

Passport services

In March 2014, the Ministry of External Affairs organised a partnership with csc special purpose vehicle (spv) to introduce passport services in the rural area through Csc include filing a passport application and paying fees, paying a fee and scheduling an appointment for a trip to a passport centre. During 2016-17, about 2.19 Lakhs passport application were submitted by csc network[5]

Plan and services

In conjunction with UIT infrastructure Technology and services Limited (UTI TSL) and National securities Depository Limited (NSDL), application for new pan card are processed by csc. Pan card service through NSDL has been introduced for csc in February 2016. During 2016-17, 28.94 Lakhs application for pan card were submitted by csc.

Clean India Campaign

In the Swach Bharat Abhiyan 2014, the government is the largest cleanliness campaign launched by the government to clean road, roads and infrastructure in 2016 the Ministry of Urban Development facilitated the creation of personalized home toilets across the country to facilitate online applications through the csc under the csc, During 2016-17, 5.26 Lakhs applications were submitted for csc network under the swach Bharat. Abroad for personalized household Toilets. When the scheme was announced the rural sanitation coverage of India was 39 per cent. The prime Minister announced a target that India be made "open-defection free when we celebrate 150th Birth anniversary of Mahatma Gandhi in 2019.[6]

The symbolism was appropriate since Gandhiji had given a lot of emphasis on Swachhata. As we have completed nearly four years of the scheme, 39 per cent rural sanitation coverage has increased to phenomenal 92 per cent. This was not an easy goal to achieve. This involved a behavioural change of the people.

Pradhan Mantri Awas Yojana

Pradhan Mantri Awas Yojana is an ambitious housing scheme of the Government for creating affordable housing units for Urban poor, Although entire Urban area of the country will be covered under the scheme the initial focus in on 500 selected cities in November 2016, a MOU was signed between Ministry of Housing and Urban poverty Alleviation (MHUPA) and csc spv for receiving PMAY application through CSC. The services are being provided by 60,000 cscs located in urban areas across states/UTS. During 2016-17 .27.97 lakhs application were filed by csc[7] network under the PMAY scheme. House competed under PM Awas yojana 178,00000 by 2019

Bharat Bill pay

Bharat bill pay is a conceptual system by the Reserve bank of India (RBI) which is run by the National payment corporation of India (NPCI). This is the one of stop bill payment platform for all bills for electricity, Mobile, broad band and landline, DTH, gas, water, etc. it is sure to ensure transaction, credibility and security.

Two primary partners for Bharat Bill pay

1. Bharat Bill payment central Unit (BBPCU) which enforces operational, technical and professional standards for the whole system and its participants, Indian National payment corporation (NPCI)act as BBPCU

2. Bharat Bill payments operating unit (BBPOU):-

   BBPOU are official operating unit according to the standards set by BBPS. BBPOUS will go to billers, aggregators and payment gateways, and customer touch points to handle bill payment through different distribution channels. After becoming csc SP. BBPO, csc can provide India Bill pay service and enable the villagers tom pay their electricity, water gas, DTH and broadband and landline post-paid bills.

Fastag by cscs

Fas tag is an electronic toll collection system in Indian by NHAI. Fasttag is an easy to use, which is reloadable tag that enable is a reloadable tag that enables automatic cut of toll charges and passes toll plaza without stopping for each transactions. The tag uses radio frequency identification (RFID) technology and after the tag is activated, the vehicle is connected to the windscreen, at present he is working in 425 toll plazas on national and state highways.

The csc Spv has partnered with NHAI to deliver fast tag through the csc network. After purchasing a digital service portal, VLE will deliver Fast tag to toll plaza, report and attach tags to the car.

FSSAI

The food safety and standards Authority of India has partnered with csc Spv to provide food business operator (FBO) registration service by the csc in July 2016. The objective of this initiative is to send a large number of registered FBS across the country with the FSSAI'S the certificate is created automatically between 2016-17, 95,603 applications for FSB registration have been submitted by csc.

Soil Health card

Farmers are issued to the farmers by the Government with the recommendations of the nutrients and fertilizers required for agriculture so that it can help improve productivity through appropriate use of input. With the launch of this scheme in 2015, the government will issue this card to 14 crore farmers.

In Dec 2016, Ministry of Agriculture and farmer welfare, signed MOU with csc spv to attach csc to soil Health card scheme. Between 2016-17, 1.24lakh Farmers have been registered through csc in 23 states.

E-District[8]

E-Districts are the Government's real life where most government to customers or G2c communications occur. The e- District project has been conceptualized to improve this exercise and to improve the performance of various department at the district level Enable and Uninterrupted distribution of civil Facilities through district administration enabled operating system automation, backend computerization and stakeholder data digitization. Department e-districts are one of 44 mission mode projects under National e-governance plan.

Service run by e-district

e-District is a government mission mode project. Under this project, high certified citizen centre services provided with the help of general services centre are being improved. Some of the services provided under this project are listed below.

Certificates:-Income Domicile, cast, birth, death, etc. creating and distributing certificates for .

1. Public distribution system (PDS):- issue of Ration card etc.
2. Social welfare scheme:-Old age pension, Family pension, widow pension, etc., distribution
3. Complaints:- Inappropriate pricing, absent teacher, availability of doctor etc.
4. RTI :- Filling and receiving information related to right to information act.
5. Linking to other e-government projects:- Registration, Land records and Driving licenses etc.
6. Utility payment:- payments for electricity, water bills, property taxes etc.
7. Other:- Arms licences, Government scheme, eligibility etc.
8. Above the all services available on the common services.

Election Commission service

The Election commission of India has partnered with cscspv, various election registration forms and EPIC printing by csc in an effort to improve enrolment in the electoral roll and to improve the data in elections to free elections.

Until then Tripura, Punjab, Chhattisgarh, Jharkhand, Bihar, Tamilnadu, Gujarat, Haryana and Maharashtra Electoral Registration Management system of the Constituencies (ERMS) has been integrated into the digital services portal. During the year 2016-17 csc has 34,780 election registration forms in these nine states, where 56.18 lakh EPICS have been printed through the csc network in these nine states.[9]

Business to Citizen (B2c)

Mobile recharge:- All the 14 telecom service providers can be made through mobile recharge digital service portal. This service is connected with telecommunication service providers so that customers can recharge their mobile real time .payments can be made through e-wallet available through digital service portal.

Mobile bill payment:- of 8 telecommunication service providers can be made through mobile bill payment Digital services portal. This service is connected with telecom service providers so that customers get mobile bill to fill real time

DTH Recharge

Dish of all six DTH operators can be done through the recharge Digital service portal (csc)

Financial Services

Digital Financial services, Awareness & Access:-

Digital Financial literacy, Particularly lack of awareness among the rural people, is a big challenge in the country, while the government is planning to release monstrous status and make India a cashless economy. Citizens, especially in rural and semi-urban area, need to create awareness about digital Financial services. "Digital Financial for rural India creating Awareness and Access through csc was launched in November 2016 csc have enabled awareness programs and various technologies with digital Finance options available for government policies and rural citizens. Digital Financial services such as IMPS, UPI, Bank, DOS Machine etc. Csc started in Spv campaign mode till march 2017. The cscs pv was given the responsibility to register 100 lakh citizens and to provide 25 lakh small traders under this programme by March 2017; the cscSpv registered more than two million people and enabled nearly 21 million businessmen.

'VLE Bazar' A rural e-commerce Venture

VLE Market is an online market platform dedicated to Unique Indian handicrafts and cottage products that are handmade, ethnic, organic and natural. Their goal is to reduce the probability of rural economy to encourage rural peoples participation in the process of shortage of civil works and low income, low productivity, informal, ineffective bodies and decision-marking the VLE market is trying to supply the gap between village artisans and urban consumers as much as necessary purchased products include specific area, specifications, local arts, modern technology and design, input elements. The VLE market aims to develop sculpted industry and explore new and commercially sustainable models of livelihood.

Skill Development

A common services centre has introduced the skill development course of the SPV:-

> Training skill to the youth in rural areas, certified them and making them eligible for suitable employment opportunities of self-employment.

Initiative under skill Development

- Skill of persons with Disabilities (PWD)
- Identifying primary Education (PMCVA) under PMKVY

CSC as GST Facility provider

The Goods and services tax (GST) is a new system of Taxation in India that has attracted many individual taxes and merged into a single tax. Constitutional Amendment Bill of 101 was presented after this constitution Act 2016. Gst is the comprehensive indirect tax on the use sale and use of goods and services in India, in exchange for taxes filled by the central and state Governments. The GST facility provider or Gsp is one of the GST systems. The tax player, Through GST facility provider, will provide all user interfaces and desktop, mobile and other interfaces communicating with GST system will be able to the csc spv has taken the lead becoming a GST facility provider. All csc across the country will serve as GST facility providers and will help the trader's to pay new taxes under the new government and will provide necessary training and support services to the people.

Banking Services

The reserve Bank of India (RBI) issued 2010 guideline to banks for financial services delivery through the csc to bring people in the rural areas along with financial inclusion. The cscspv has so far partnered with 42 public and private sector banks and regional rural bank to take advantage of last-mile network to bring non-affiliated, especially coastal communities and women to banking. Under this partnership, business correspondent agent/ customer service points can be made to deliver banking facility to the csc in the country such as:- Account opening manual- Account opening (e- KYC) Deposit money, withdrawn, Balance inquiries, Recurring/Fixed Deposits etc.

During 2016-17 banking services of 36 bank-23 PUS banks and 13 rural Bank services have been made available through 11,940 Business correspondent agent/customer service points across the country .During the financial year, Transactions of Rs.382.71 Lakh. This BC has made 5.70.163.61 lakhs.[10]During 2016-17, 126309 VLEs are registered under the Digital services about 28.351 lakh successful transactions were conducted in the public service under Dig pay 17.901.89 million.

Insurance Service

Common services centre spv bought license from insurance Regulatory and Development Authority (IRDA) in 2013 to operate as a authorized intermediary for market life and non-life insurance products through VLEs. The csc started giving general, health and life insurance policies to rural investors to rural customers.. So far, 36 insurance policies through csc .The csc has introduced motor third party insurance to rural customers.

Jan Suraksha Yojana

The government started three special insurance and pension schemes for citizens in 2015, especially from unorganized sector and marginal communities. VLEs working as Business and customer agents can offer three social security plans –Pradhan Mantri Suraksha Bima Yojana (PMSBY), Prime Minister Jyoti BimaYojana and Atal pension Yojana to the citizens. Punjab National Bank agrees to increase the APY registration of its account holders by the csc nationwide.

Pension Services

The National pension system (NPS) is voluntary, defined contribution retirement saving plan designed to enable customers to make optimum decision by making systematic savings during their decision-making life. NPS is making efforts to save citizens retirement habits. It is an attempt to find permanent solutions to the problem of providing adequate retirement income to every citizen of India. Since April 2017, the NPS service has been started by the csc.

Pradhan Mantri Fasal BimaYojana

PMFBY is a comprehensive income-based crop insurance plan of the government that provides financial assistance to the victims of crop loss/damage arising out of objective incidents. This scheme has caused crop damage:-

Prevent solving/planting:-Or ought, floods, inflammation, pests and diseases, natural fire and electricity, storms, etc.

Local Disaster- Fasal Bima has started in 2017 due to hailstorm, ground slide, and rain-harvesting Fasal Bima for Farmers through the cscspv network in partnership with Bajaj Allianz General Insurance company with this scheme, many farmers are getting help so the farmers are very happy and are trying to make their lives better. Number of formers resister under PM fasal Bima yojana 529,56443 by November 2019

Education services

Today education services are also being provided by digital services centres. They are as follows:-

National Digital Literacy Mission Dhisha (NDLM)

Round about 30 per of the population lives below the poverty line in India literacy rate is more than 25-30 per and the percentage of digital literacy is in the Units figures. Although the desire to become part of the replication of the people of rural India is increasing. The Government has started the National Digital literacy Mission programme to make India digitally literate. The goal of this programme is not only to create digital literacy, awareness and active awareness, but also to impart education and capacity programmes. It is aimed to helping rural communities play leading role in the global digital economy and maintain competitiveness, and can also shape technically empowering society.

Under the Ministry of Communication and Information technology, Department of electronics and information technology (Deity) launched a scheme for first phase of the programme, National Digital literacy mission (NDLM) was launched in August 2014.

In the select blocks of each state / UT providing literacy to 10 million people, one person from every digital illiterate house. The second phase of the programme known as Digital shaksarta Abhiyan will being in December 2014 with the aim of providing digital literacy training to 42.50 lakhs citizens was done Grassroots government workers and authorized ration dealers like Asha and Anganwadi workers were also included under this scheme. The cscspv achieved target under the NDML Disha scheme by October 2016, the project timeline is much ahead more than 100 lakhs citizens are registered for digital literacy training out of which 87.68 lakhs are trained and 53.46 lakh are certified.

Training partners 624, Registered candidates 18872029,and Training completed 177747333, certified students in across India and Maharashtra status is a 4944.99 student certified total District, only Nanded District status 22979 student is registered, training completed student 21805 certified student 10261[11] Above status that the bye day.

Pradhan Mantri Gramin Digital Sakshtrata Abhiyan

(PMGDISHA): following the successful execution of the NDLM –Disha scheme, the Indian Government launched a new digital literacy scheme in 8 February 2017 in particular targeting the countries [12]PradhanMantriGramin digital Saksharta Abhiyan provides digital literacy training to six crore citizens in rural Areas, so that 40 per of the rural households in each Digital unskilled households reach 40 per rural households. The csc is working for the spv scheme.

Cyber Gram Yojana

The cyber Gram Yojana is part of multi-sectoral development programme (MSDP) Through Minority affairs under this programme, the students of minority, Communities, especially girls of Madras, have basic digital literacy training. During the year 2016-17 the project was implemented in four states of west Bengal, Uttar Pradesh, Tripura and Rajasthan, during this period, 1.88 Lakh Madras students are registered under this programme out of which 1.55 lakh are trained and 1.43 lakh are certified.

BBC Course:- in an effort to achieve basic computer literacy, cscspv has provided basic computer, Computer courses with emphasis on basic training. The programme prepares someone for thc use of Computers in business and personal space. National institute of open schooling service has partnered with cscspv to provide facilities for students. Under this partnership, csc can open school education in rural india.

Introduction to GST

Tally has introduced a new course on 'GST introduction' through the csc platform on GST. This course is useful for any citizens whom want to update their Knowledge on GST.

Government Examination:-There is an online forum to help students prepare for both state and central government exams in the state examination.

Health Services

Tele-health Consultation:- The greek word "tele" meaning "distance" and the latin word mederi meaning "to heal" telemedicine is the type of primary care were the patient has demanded a doctor's advice about emergency medical problems, which does not require a doctor's appointment when he or she needs a face to face will not consult, but they will csc is providing video-based teleconsultation services across India to make grassroots access to health care consultation service throughout India at affordable rates. CSC spv Apollo Hospitals limited has approved a telephone consultation with Apollo Hospitals doctor in 2014. In 2016 the csc spv started the entire tale-health consulting service through all India age, Homeopathic and Ayurvedic doctors all over the country.

Pradhan Mantri Jan Aushadhi Yojana

The objective of Pradhan Mantri Jan Aushadhi Yojana is to provide quality medicines at affordable prices to the poor and the deprived people, especially through exclusive outlets called Jan Aushadhi Medical stores. This scheme is implemented by pharmaceutical public sector undertaking cscspv established generic medicinal stores in January 2015 with BPPI in the Jan AushadhiYojana of csc across the country.

Jiva Ayurvedic Scheme

Cscspv has made Ayurveda advocacy and more than 150 Ayurvedic products to bring citizens through the csc Network. "The service was launched in July 2016 in Haryana, Uttar Pradesh, and Panjab Jiva is now directly producing Ayurvedic production sale is now live in Maharashtra Madhya Pradesh, West Bengal apart b from northern India state.

E-Signature Service

To create electronic signatures, the indicator must obtain Digital signature Certificate (DSC) from the certifying Authority licensed by the controller Certified Authority under Information Technology Act 2000, it is essential to adopt a large number of citizen services, digital signatures on paper completely, it is easy touse online services to give everyone the ability to digitally sign electronic network. CSC CA is set to meet the requirement for issuing digital signature certificates for the e-sign service.

E-sign is an online electronic signature service that can be combined with service delivery application e-sign users to digitally sign documents. Using the e-sign users Authentication through the e-KYC service the online electronic signatures service is facilitated, reliable and secure alternative to saving e-papers through this service Digital Locker, e-filing, Financial sector, account opening in bank and post office, Driving licences renewal, birth, Death, cast etc. Five e-signature service providers to provide digital service like certification 5.89 corers e-signature services have been given.[13]

All the above digital services are now being transparency accessible to all the citizens are satisfied with this service, saving time and money.

Other important mechanism for effective Administration

1. Umang (Unified Mobile Application for New-age Governance)

Umang provides a single platform for all India citizens to access PAN India e-Governance services in central to local government institution and other citizen-centric service.

Umang is developed by ministry of electronics e-Governance Division to drive Mobile Governance in India.

The aim is provide Major services provided by central organisation and local Government Departments, local bodies and other Utility services from private organisations. It provides a Unified approach where citizens can install an application, web IVR and SMS which can be accessed through smartphones, feature phones, tablets. Umang has been created with a through to add convenience to your lifestyle.

Important Features:-

- Umang provides seamless integration with popular customer-focused services such as Aadhar and Digilocker.
- It provides a Unified approach where you can install an application to get multiple government services.
- Umang can be accessed on a number of channel like mobile apps, web, IVR and sms which can be acceded through smartphones, tablets, and desktop.
- Umang has a rich multimedia interface that will focus on enhancing utility an enriching users experience.
- Umang supports 12 Major Indian languages in addition to English.

Through the Umang application more than 67 Department and 334 Government services can be availed by the present government, with the help of the same technology, the aim of making available has been fixed.[14]This services has given common citizen the services to their nearest locations 50 they satisfied.

(2) JeevanPraaman

JeevanPraaman is a biometric capable digital service for pensioners. Pensioners of central Government, state Government or any other government organisation can take advantage of this facility this scheme was launched on Nov 10, 2014. Beneficiaries of this scheme are the retired government and PSU employee.

After retirement an important requirement for pensioners is to give life certificates to the agencies in respect of authorized pension distribution agencies such their pension is credited to their account, For obtaining this life certificate a pensioners is required to personally submit himself to the pension distribution agency of before he has served and a life certificate issued by the authority sent to the distributer agency is necessary.

By using the standard of life, the pensioners can now present evidence of his existence to the authorities in order to continue the pension for the fulfilment of the life certificate issued by his or her physical authority.

This government service is arranged to get pension payments directly from the senior citizen through the Aadhar number and the payment of the document is made in the direct bank. From 2014 to till today this service has been distributed by 1.73 crores of certificates.[15]

1. DigiLocker

Digilocker is one of the Key initiatives of Digital India programme which enables an individual to have and access its dedicated personal storage space associated with each resident base number. Digitalize can be used to secure e-documents and to secure e-Resource identifier (URI) links issued by various issuing department. The e-sign facility provided as part of the Decelerator system can be used for digital signature on e-documents. Access through digital web portal or mobile application. Number of documents issued through Digilocker 7.76 Billion by Aug. 2024.

Digilockers main Components:-

Each residents digital account has the following sections:_

1. **Dash board**:- The first page this page appears when you log in and show a summary of all your documents.
2. **Issue Document**:- This section displays the VRI (s) of documents or certificates issued by the government. Department or other agency participating in the developer.

3. **Uploaded Document**:- This section displays all documents uploaded by you. You can update the document type, e-sign and share this uploaded documents.

4. **Shared Documents**:- This section shows you a list of shared documents. (by e-mail)

5. **Activity:-**There is a long of activity made in this section of Digilocker accounts.

6. Upload files to logs download, e-sign, etc.

7. **Issuers:-** The department and agencies issued in this section are listed which are registered on the Digitalize. If these departments have issued a documents / Certificate to you, it will appear in the form of a URI (link) in your issued document section.

This service launched by the Prime Minister on 1 July 2015. In July 2016 digilocker recorded 20.13 lakhs users with a repository of 24.13 lakhs documents. The April when the Government had urged all municipal bodies to use Digilocker to make their administration paperless.[16]

Rahuri Nagar parishad in Ahmednagar district of Maharashtra became the first municipal council to get the status of integration with digital locker for implementation of all the necessary documents. This service was started on 28th April 2016 as part of the Digital India Programme.[17]

Todays every India's district, state, Village are trying to make paper less administrative offices using Digital locker, this is the result of Digital India programme.

Digital payment system

In India various tools are being used for digital payment, like Bank cards, Unstructured supplementary service data (USSD) based Mobile banking, Aadhar enable payment system (AEPS), unified payment interface, wallets, point of sale and various Mobile apps on Digital payment etc.

Most important tools for study are:-

1. **Bharat Interface for Money (BHIM)**

Bharat Interface for money (Bhim)is a mobile application developed by National payments corporation of India (NPCI) based on the unified payment interface (UPI) it was launched by Prime Minister Narendra Modi, at Digidhanmela at talkatorastadium in New Delhi on 30 December 2016.

It was named after **Dr.B.R. Ambedkar** and is intended to facilitate e-payments directly through books as part of the 2016 Indian banknote demonetisation and drive towards cashless transactions. BHIM apps initial release 14 April 2017. This apps currently supports is languages (including English) The Bhim app is only a mechanism which transfer money between different bank accounts. Transaction on Bhim are nearly simultaneous and can be done 24/7 and use to check the current balance in their bank accounts and to choose which account to use for conducting transaction.

There is huge increase in Digital payment practices 2014-15 in in years, 316 Crore financial transactions were made through digital, in 2017-18, 2017crore transactions were made through Digital technology. New options to sophisticated technology like bharat interface for money, rupay debit card etc. are also every easy to use today many people across the country using digital technology for various financial transaction such as sending money, taxing, paying service fees etc. Till September 2018, more than 78948 crore financial transaction has been made through Bhim apps. In a very short time the usefulness of the bhim apps, popularly known among young Indian savvy smartphone holders is being praised worldwide today .More and more people use these apps to send money, to purchase money, to accept money. In September 2018 more than 48 crore of rupees were borrowed through the Bhim apps.[18]

After studying the above digital administration system it appears that the importance of digital Administration in today's era is increasing day to day. Through this digital Administration our country seems to be corruption free, transparent and accountable.

Digital kranti in Maharashtra

In today's digital era, Maharashtra is recognized as the leading state of Maharashtra for various administrative reforms.

i-Sarita:-(Stamp and Registration Information Technology Administration)

Registry and stamp department deals with some important events in one's life. This includes purchase and sale of immovable property. Stamp duty Marriage registration and such activities, it is estimated that about 2 crore people are availing services in the department every year.

Sarita is a G2C project for the preparation development and implementation of computerized application for registration of documents received at each G Register office and to provide data update from time to the concerned District Register and senior offices subject to the department. In the last few years the department has made significant changes in the documenting process. A computerized system of Sarita was started for the registration of Documents in 2002. In the year 2012 with a new well connected network to centralize the whole administration and implementation of the registration process. isarita is a web based application developed by Nic which connects the 480. Sub Register offices in the state of Maharashtra.[19] It is a step forward from more computerization of data to complete digitization of registration process. Wherein all the data collected during registration process at any sub register offices is saved to the central server.

Services Offered

1. Registration of 67 different types of documents required by the government.
2. Extensive software networked on 360 sites has been deployed simultaneously.
3. Document with all relevant parameters are registered and distributed to people in less than 30 minutes. Error free registration with online monitoring and document encryption with photographs of seller buyer and complainants and fingerprint
4. Production in narrow hidden form for easier reactions and administration on the site Registration- Evaluation scan-archive, networking and process monitoring integration.

'AapaleSarakar' Poratal

AapaleSarakar is a web portal that means Digital Maharashtra is one step towards Maharashtra. This effort has been started under the Digital Maharashtra Campaign in the state. It is an attempt to provide service to the people using the technology. The state government has announced as a digital year 2015, hence it has adopted the digital file on the Ministry. Given a definite time for this. On January 26, 2015 the information and technology Department of Maharashtra has given the new portal 'AapaleSarakar' for the people of Maharashtra. Chief Minister Devendra Fadnavis had promised to launched web portal within 100 days to welcome and participate in the administration of public instruction in his party manifesto Apart from this on the 9th January in Bharatiya pravasi divas program, he had promised to launched a web portal 'AapaleSarakar' for direct communication. This web portal will be used as medium to communicate effectively to the public and the government. This portal will be working for the Ministry level department. After this extension will be done at regional and district levels. A new revolution started through this web portal according, on January 26, the web portal was released.

AapaleSarakar web portal is an online system that connects the people directly to the Ministry of the state. This is a medium of double communication through mobile and computer and the government fulfils liability towards the public in this regard through giving response this portal will be controlled by the Chief Minister's Office. The guarantee of the contest is the portal feature.

Feature of web portal

Reporting of this web portal, filing of information and supporting innovative instructions are three important parts. However, this is another feature of this web portal. What is the process that will be done on your application; through the tracking Report will be known. This web portal containing phases will be divided into divisions, districts and Taluka's level is scheduled to start.

The Structure of the web Portal 'AapaleSarakar'

Important components have been included in this web portal

Grievance redressed:- The citizen can file his grievance under the appropriate category. After that, the applicant will get the token number of the complaint filed. Use the number to know the current status of the complaint.

Right to Information:- The application for the Ministry's department or the first appeal will be paid using the internet banking/ debit card /Credit card.

Co-operation:- In order to promote the concept of good governance and to increase participation in public administration, this section of the portal will be used to get in formation and feedback about the Government's.

Right to Public service Act

The Maharashtra Right to Public service Act, 2015 is a revolutionary Act. This Act provides that the peoples shall be provided services by the Maharashtra government in a transparent, efficient, effectively and time bound manner, in order to ensure effective implementation of this Act, the Maharashtra state commission for Right to service has been established. This commission is headed by the state chief Commissioner for Right to service Shri. Swadneen Kshatriya, who was formally Chief Secretary of the Maharashtra State.[20]

People can get complete information regarding which services are available under this Act by accessing either the Mobile app RTS Maharashtra or 'AapaleSarakar' web portal. People can similar apply online for availing these services or denial of the services without sufficient Justification, Citizens can file first Appeal and second Appeal with senior officers within the department and third and final Appeal can be filed before this commission.

Maha Schemes

The Maha Schemes has been created with the information available to the government on a single platform. Citizens will get information about various schemes information about various issues such as government decision, eligibility criteria, application process, required documents, time to get benefit, related officers etc. A part form this, the information about Regional offices and Officers in each division and information on the telephone number is available on the website. It is possible for the citizen to know the plan and contact the appropriate officer and the office by preparing the necessary preparation for the benefit on the scheme. This will save you a lot of time and effort.

Included various Departments likes Agriculture Department, Animal husbandry, Dairy Development, Fisheries, Co-operation, Textile, Skill development, environment, Food, Civil supplies and Consumer protection, General Administration Department, Higher Technical education, Home-transport and ports, Housing, Law and Judiciary, planning, public health, Revenue-forest, Rural, School education, Social Justice and special assistance, water Resources, water supply and sanitation, women and child welfare Department etc.[21]

Management and work method

There will be a responsible officer for each department. This officer will be responsible for monitoring the issue of redressed of grievances on the web portal of your government on this portal, citizens can register their complaint online using mobile number and e-mail address in case of online registration, get access. Public grievances of citizens will be resolved in maximum twenty one days. The maximum limit will be taken by the administration in six month from the time of 'ApaleSarakar' portal from seven days of its execution. After the grievances are resolved through the government, the citizen will receive the message and the feedback will be asked Improvements will be made on the web portal.

These complaints will not be accepted

Complaints about the matters of Judicial proceeding or in which the Judgements are expected to be judged, personal and family disputed which have not been filled in the Taluka, Sub-divisional, district-level appropriate authorities and complaints regarding the Right to information application cannot be filed on the web portal.

Methods to use for citizens

To go to 'AapleSarakar' web portal visit www.aapale sarakar. maharashtra.gov.in this web portal is a available in Marathi and English is available in Marathi and English languages. There are five icons highlight in front of the home screen on this website. The five (icon) department is involved in Right to information, my Gov. (for suggestion/ feedback), and Maha schemes, etc. Enter any of those department who want to interact with the government. Your mobile number and e-mail address are only required to respond. For example, redressed of grievances in this section once you file a complaint, your tracking number will be ready. Through this number you can see the current information regarding getting the right information. Online is made in the second part online payment facility is a featured of this department. Third section is of co-operation:- This is part of the government to give suggestion and innovative ideas to the government for sensitive citizens it has six sections in structures have been issued in six sections of Youth Maharashtra, Drought free Maharashtra, Tourism, Digital Maharashtra and clean Maharashtra. However, other ideas can be projected in 500 words. Direct contact with chief Minister can be done from this place.

The First State to have an Online RTI Act

Maharashtra has become the first state in the history of the web portal. Court fee stamps were required to be used when using this law. Now you can pay the fees required by your bank account using internet banking/debit card/credit card. The right to information under all be administrative divisions can be used here. The departments list is also made available at this place.

A Step towards Digital Maharashtra

The web portal 'AapaleSarakar' is a step towards digitized Maharashtra. Good governance is possible through transparency and mobility. This effort has been started under the Digital Maharashtra Campaign in the state. This is an attempt to provide services to the public using technology. The state government has announced 2015 as a digital year.[22] so now the files will be accepted level for this a fixed date will be decided, then files other than e-files will not be accepted. Digital Services in Maharashtra are being provided by 'AapaleSarakar' portal. It has become the government of the old setu facilitation centre and now it has become our government. All the people of the state are getting digital services i.e. citizens are satisfied with this success due to this success every Grampanchyat your government service centre. The citizen facility centre will be completed within a few days of course there is the goal of the state government, which aims to centre no doubt about it.

Digital Satbara (7/12) (Digital Administration, transparent Administration)

After registering the purchase documents of the sub-Registrar to the Registrar it is necessary to rectify it and them after removing the notice, it is necessary for some time to make the talathi office weary. Talathi is not available for two to three villages at the same time. Due to the inconvenience of the resulting citizen, it becomes had decided to implement the e-Chawadi program by compiling the talathi offices and to make it more easily accessible to the citizens. Under this initiative, entire seven day computerization of the district was done. During computerization the error talathi office has been corrected.

According to the Sub-Divisional officer

After registering the procurement dump for the online service, he will get immediate information in his mutation cell at the tehasil office immediately after the entry of the information, and then it will be ready for the next seven years. The notice will not be removed from them, it has been changed in fifteen days but it will not get any problem in the next 15 days. The Revenue Act has also been changed to avoid issuing notice to those who have been present for the registration of the stamp, which has been closed for seven year. Every farmer has to see his Stbara Government at http://mahabhulekh.maharashtra,gov.in. Farmers can also see their own accounts in this place. If the farmers get any mistakes in these seven or more accounts. They should contact the concerned authorities immediately.

After the special campaign for salaried reading, the account correction process is effectively 7/12 and 8-A account holders is there a need for spelling repairs in the name, which accounts need to be partitioned? A list of such accounts is being prepared after that the work of the Account master is being done. In order to amend repairs of 7/12, published in chavadi reading and to correct some of the reports from 1to 26, first 7/12 corrections are being made, the first list is being prepared. After such repairs and after repairs, it is being investigated by the Board officer naib Tahsildar, Tahsildar, Deputy Collector and collector. If there are any errors in the inspections they are also being corrected. The Tehsildar has sent inquiry report of 24 officials of the revenue officers and the revenue administration is prepared to ensure the exact 7/12 and 8(A) to the account holders by ensuring that they received the 7/12 inspection certificate of the form and revenue officer, staff.[23]

E-rectification

In the state the centrally sponsored Digital India land records Modulation program (DILRMP) is being implemented and National information centre, Pune has developed e-modification programs.

Manuscript Right records to very exactly the computerized rights archive, the confirmed authority records have been read by the Edit module and the proper computerized authority records have been read. The functioning of the Edit Module of Dhule district is 97.22 percent. Manuscript reports in Dhule district have been closed completely and in Shirpur and Shindkhed atalikas, e-rectification process is being implemented for last two years whereas in Dhule and Sakari talulas e-revision has been done for last one year. So far, 51 thousand 941 such records have been made through e-modification programme in Dhule.

Experience of the Dynamic Administration due to online Documents

Examples of senior citizens living with domicile nationality are now getting online and this has made citizens feel like a dynamic administration. Digital signature certificates have been distributed online. This has resulted in the feeling of the administration of the people due to the saving of money with the timing of citizens, with the help of online method of eliminating revenue claims, helping people with a large number of government help is eliminated. Through this system, the result of filing and hearing of citizens time are available to the citizens for the time being saved with the introduction of the tehsildar, Naib-Tehsildar, along with the tehsildars, revenue tribunal cases are being simplified by online system to go to www.edisnic.gov.in website citizens can see information about your case.[24]

Nanded District of Maharashtra has become completely digital, so all activities of the revenue department appear to be done digitally.

So that people are satisfied with the service of the government and there is transparency in the administration due to the end of corruption. As well as farmers of the state Satbara will be connected directly to the Aadhar card. After checking the thumb impression of any farmer, the data will be verified from the information base of the Talathi office. The same information will be used for further processing of bank, insurance companies, crop production, crop harvesting and sale of land.

The state government is continuously trying to reduce the investigation done by the Talathi offices of the state. The government is not the sole purpose of distributing it only on online and distribution. Now for applying for registration of application, heirs, record of losses, death certificate or application for reciprocity online application is not available at the talathi office senior sources in the revenue department said that the revenue department has said talathi office is a very important part of the farmers for the farmers of the state. Talathi is working on the work of village level work, and farmers have to go to the Talathi office for various work. Farmers are ineligible due to various reasons like bribery, delay, mistakes and absence. Therefore the state government is in the process of bringing all activities online in the future.

Reference

1. E-governance policy initiatives under Digital India, published report, Department of electronic and information technology, government of India. (Page no. 10)
2. Common service centres, Ministry of electronics and information technology, government of India. (page no. 7)
3. https://transformingIndia. My.gov.in/per form dashboard/primary
4. Sanjeev Mittal, e-governance in rural India. article in Kurukshetra (Aug 2017) Journal, Ministry of rural Development Gov. of India,(page no. 9)
5. https://csc.gov.in/government to citizen.
6. Arun Jaitlye, a people's movement Article published in Yojana (Nov-2018) government of India.(page no. 7)
7. https://Pmay.com/current status
8. https://Vikaspedia.in /e-governance/e-district/mission mode project
9. https://csc.gov.in /government to citizen.
10. https://csc.gov.in/Financial inclusion.
11. https://Pmg disha.in/students/counts-list/
12. Chandra Bhushansharma, innovation in technology supported Distance learning, published Articles in Kurukshetra Journal (Dec2018) Gov. of India (page. no. 29)
13. Prasad, Ravishankar. (Dec.2018) *Digital The aim of empowering*. Article published in Yojana Journal, govt. of. India, page no. 8.
14. https://webumang.gov.in/web/#
15. Prasad, Ravishankar. (Dec.2018) *Digital The aim of empowering*. Article published in Yojana Journal, govt. of India, page no. 7.
16. Pranavmukul, digilocker initiative record repository of 24.13 lakh does from 2013, the Indian express, dated-06.10.2017.
17. https://vikaspedia.in/e governance/best practices/rahuri in ahemednager/first to have digilocker

18. ibid, 13. page 07
19. A. K. Srinivas and other, case studies on department of registration and stamp: project sarita, NeG plan page 05.
20. https/aaplesarkar.mahaonline.gov.in/en/commonform/atsact.
21. Ibid, 20.
22. https://mr.vikaspedia.in/e-governance/online citizen/services/92e93993e.
23. https://mahabhulekh.maharashtra.gov.in.
24. https://edisnic.gov.in/dynanic administration.

Chapter - 4

Impact and Implement of Digital Administration

Introduction

In the previous chapter, Mechanism of digital administration was studied, it is necessary to use the impact of digital Administration in Nanded district, because the area of research is in Nanded district, to study the digital administration of it, related officers, employees of the digital administration in Nanded district, Operators of CSC,s Apple sarkar, setu facilitation canter, and related. Citizens of the study were to compile the basis of questionnaires filled for data by creating a separate questionnaire for each of the selected reference as stockholders. In this chapter, the matter was completed based on its explain action Presentation, thought the table, graphs And diagrams etc. Today, in order to implement the e-governance policy in Maharashtra, the government is trying to digitize each district by implementing e-Governance project and today the Nanded district is providing digital services to officers, employees, by the revenue department and the CSC Apple sarkar, e-suvidua Centre is giving digital services to citizens. Hence citizens of Nanded district are also moving towards the digital era.

Nanded District at a Glance

The history of Nanded district has been long since. Nanded was formerly known as 'Nanditat[1] which was confirmed by the copper plates found at was him. Nanded is mentioned in the book Lilacaritra written by Mahambantta 700 year ago. It gives information about Narsinghs's idol in the city. It is said that pandavas of Mahabharata during puranic period traveled through Nanded District. The great successor the Nanded dynasty ruled. The rulers of the Nand Dynasty ruled from generation to generation about the first century. Andhra Benda or satvahan dynasty ruled from Nanded district and the surrounding area. In the fourth century Kandahar was the capital of sogadev. According to the inscription of Krishkadev alis kharadev at tekhandar a Rashtrakut. King was also established in Kandahar. Another inscription in Arhapur shows that some clan Rashtrakutas were ruling in devlur. A place in Nanded District, was the capital of the Hotal, Chalukya dynasty, and after kakatiya dynasty there was a kingdom of yadvas of Diva Geri, which was the last hindu dynasty to rule over this kingdom after first invasion of Muslims, this region become Subject to them and after some year they become the chief of malik kafur, al-ud- din khilji. The arrival the bahamani dynasty, or suthorn country.

The deccan was divided into four parts or subhas, and Nanded was included in the wellbeing of Telangana. by splittimg the kingdom Mahmud ghavan, the famous wazir or the bahmamis of bahmamis, ruled the subhash with the nanded port of the mahabharata Baghghat. He spent mamy days at nanded and kandhar and established wazirabad portion of nanded city. Nanded was the capital of Telangana District during this period: aurangzebala dkakan was oppoimted as the headmaster while the headquarters of Bidder Subha and he was known as Ahmedabad. This shubh bider was divied into six governments and 76 mahals and was one of the governments of Nanded ki Shubha. in 1708 after Aurangzebs death, his son his spiritual leader guru Gobind singh, came to Nanded in his permanent residence. It was like this that they had preached in Sikhism that they do not need any spiritual leader and they should take the panth as their leader. amonument is contracted in one place where he breathes his last breath. A gurudwara is also built there He is known as takhat sachkhand shri hajoor Achchalnager Sahib Gurudwara.

ItbecamepartHyderabadin1725whentheNizamchosepermanently and continued till 1947.[2] When india obtained independence and took police action against Hyderabad and Hyderabad, Hyderabad become a part the marathwada region of Hyderabad state and become part of the bilingaual Bombay state and as a result of Maharashtra's creation, district has be com part or Maharashtra state.

Nandgiri Fort

As a witness to the ancient Nanded of the Nand regime Holi Nandgiti situated on the nortnern bank of the Goddess Bhuikont fort. This is Nandedkar's fate earlier; The entire village was situated in the fort and proved to be found on th for tifications found in the fort. The special feature of this fort is that the eastern and south sides of the Godavari flow due to which there is no moat around the Bhuikot. The fort of 28 acres are is found in the ruins of two beaches of east and south side the bastion is an important component of this fort, 14 km from the outer fort and 14 in the interior of the fort from 19 to the total of 33 to wers, this fort has the magnitude grandeur and fortitude Nanded has great cultural heritage also it is the placc of thc birth of saint poets like vishnupant sesa, Raghunath sesa and pandit besides being a contre for learning Sanskrit. that's why Sanskrit poet is also known as the district.[3]

Geographical location

Nanded is the second big city in marathwada. The geographical location shows that the city is located 18°. 15' to 19°. 55' and East longitude of 77°. 7 to 78.° 25 about 10,522 59 Sq km. the district is speed over the area Nanded is on the south eastern part of Maharashtra. This part is composed of southern Bidar district of Karnataka, Nizamabad district of Andrapradesh and Adilabad district in south east, Yavatmal District in the north and Parbhani district in North – West and Latur district in southeast.

This Nanded district is geographically divided in to two main parts. The mountainous region is in the two main parts, the mountainous region is in the northern and eastern parts of Godawari vallery, The rest is in the southern part or the rest is in the southern part or the vally spread over the edge of various rivers like Godavari, Penganga, Manshera, and maniyad.[4]

There are 16 Talukas in Nanded Distric such as Ardhapur, Kinwat, Bhoker, Loha, Biloli, Mahoor, Degloor, Mukhed, Dharmadad, Mudkhed, Hadgaon, Nanded, Himayatnagar, Naigon (KH) Kandhar, Umari.

Population

According to the 20011 census Nanded's population are 3,361,292. Male are 17,30,075 and female are 16,31217. According to the 2001 census Nanded had a population of 2,876,259 its Nanded district has a population of 2.99 % of the total population of Maharashtra.

According to the 2001 census, there was change of 16.86 percent compared to the population.[5]

Literacy

Literacy rate of Nanded district is 75.45 percent. Male litarcy rate is in 84.27% and female literacy rate is 66.15 percent.[6]

Education

There are a total of 504 High Schools. (Secondary & sr. secondary school) in Nanded District.

One Sawami Ramanand Teerth Marathwada University, Nanded, Attached Colleges, near about 250 (including arts, Commerce, Science, Education, Law medial, Engineering etc.)

Transport

Nanded District is well Connected with Various part of the country through railways, uses and. Airways and roadways.

Tourism

(1) **Guirudwara:-** The takht sachkhand Shri Huzur Abchalnager Sahib is the main Grudwara of nanded this grudwars Build by Maharaja Ranitising (Meanwhile 1830 to 1839) and other seven (7) Grudwara's are building Nanded. Likes- Naginga Ghat, Bandhaghat, sangat sahib, Maltekdi, Hira Hat, Shikar Ghat Mata Rahib Devanji.

(2) **Mahurgad:-** It is an ancient village situated on the sahyadri mountains, on the edge of painganga Devotees of pilgrimage pilgrimage area. Mahuragad is a complete and original the Goddess's three and a half original verse. The tample of goddess renuka Devi is situated in Mahur Taluka.

(3) **Hottal:-** There is a very beautiful temple at Hottal of lord Siddheshwara which is known for the art of the chlukya Era.

Mahavihar, Bavari Nager (A holy pilgrimage zone) Near Mahavihar, Bavrinagar Taluka Arjapur Dist. Nanded. The All India Buddhist Dhamma, parishad is organized internationally Dhamma parishad annually in ponsh purnima. Great Solitaire and Great organizer Dr. S.P. Gaikwad is her organizer. Dr. Gaikwad's this holy the word and the ancient heritage of Nanded – another precious jewel in the treasury. 8 january 2004 Raja Due to the historical importance of Bavaria. In front of the quiet and vast mass of people whe are concertrated in the 17th all India budhist conference here then chier Minister Sushilkumar shinde declared Mahavihara, Bavarinagar as sacred pilgrim center. Later on 4th June 2004 the declaration was made in the government decision Not only this government has also proposed the proposed plan for development of this area.[7]

Social and Economic condition

Socio – economic status of Nanded district was not so satisfying nizam period, wealth and financial strength, some landlords. Nawab etc. the people of the Nizam period were the sources of income social like has affected people's lives due to limited. They were deprived Education, health care, etc. But when Maharashtra became a state the Government of India is focused on the socio- economic development of people in the district, even though the socio-economic development of nanded District is comparatively less than other parts of Maharashtra such as kokan and western state the reson for the comparatively less socio economic development of the people in Nanded district than other parts of Maharashtra is that Nanded District was ruled by the Nizam where as other parts of Maharashtra were ruled made by Britisher.[8]

Nanded District Administrative set up

Maharashtra static is divided into several divisions for the vantage or Administration the divisions are follows:-

(1) Konkan Division

(2) pune Division

(3) Nashik Division

(4) Aurangabad Division

(5) Amravati Division

(6) Nagpur Division

The Aurangabad division consists of Aurangabad, Beed, Jalna, Parbhani, Latur, Hingoli, Osmanabad, and Nanded districts.

Nanded district is divided in to 16 talukas under 08 revenue sub-Division, Tahsil offices 16 and Talathi Saja 84 revenues circle 14 total Village 1603 The Under each Sub division are as following.

Sub- Division in Nanded District

Sr.no	Bub-Divisions	Talukas
1.	Nanded	Nanded, Ardhapur.
2.	Bhokar	Bhokar, Mudkhed.
3.	Biloli	Biloli, Naigaon.
4.	Degloor	Dharmadad, Umri.
5.	Dharmabad	Dharmabad, Umri.
6.	Hadgaon	Hadgaon Himayat Nagar
7.	Khandar	Khandhar, Loha.
8.	Kinwat	Kinwat, Mahur.

Source:- https:nanded.gov.in/subdivision-blocks/

For studying the digital administration between the department of each division from the total eight sub division of Nanded district officers and employees, cscs /aplesarkar centers operator and citizens. Respectively 10,10,15 as Sample of total 35 respondent from a division, the total (8) eight sub divisions in Nanded district that is why 8 X 35 = 280 respondents selected for this present research, the data have been collected by the same reply respondents through the questionnaire scheduled, as shown in the following.

DATA ANALYSIS INTERPRETAION

The analysis and interpretation of the data was node with reference to the research problem and objectives of the study and statement of the hypothesis to be tested analysis and inter predation of data. Researcher used table, graphs and diagrams wherever necessary, for these purpose relevant experts' guidance and opinion are also sought to analyze the data wherever required.

Internet Connectively in Administration

After Studying whether the administrative office is connected with internet or not?, it has been found that the office has been found to have computers and internet connectivity with the information received from the respondent selected by the sample and the actual survey and actual observation because the entire respondents (100%) says that all computers are connected with internet in administrative offices, it has been proven.

Therefore, today, every office has a lot of need for internet service; only then the work of every citizen can be completed within a time. All the offices have been found to have computer and internet connectivity.

Speed of work

How digital services speed up the administrative services? Such as question to respondents, while 92.5 % of respondents says that Digital service speed is fast, 05 % of respondents says that Digital service speed is slow, lastly 2.5 % of respondents says that time consuming due to Digital services in administrative offices.

This study it is clear that the functioning of the office due of digital administration is fast, but somewhat administrative officers facing various problems.

Impact on administration

What impact did the digital service have on administration? The question asked by researcher to respondents, the mostly 65% respondents say that there was transparency in the administration due to digital services while 27.5 % respondent says that administrative work is prompt due to Digital services. After that the lowest 7.5% respondent says that corruption has decreased in administration.

It is clear explained that digital administration has made transparency in the administration, but corruption seem to have not been completely reduced.

Use of tools in Administration

To study the tools used when giving digital services to administration which tools do you for digital services? When asked such a question to respondents the highest 71.25% respondent said that computer used for the digital services in administration, after that the 16.25% respondents says the administration is using a Laptop for digital service, and 10% respondents says that mobile phones are used when giving digital services in administration, while the lowest 2.5% respondents say that they use other tools other than them.

It is clear explain that when using digital services in administration it is seen that the use of computer is of greater use of computers is of greater use.

Internet Connectivity in Administration

To study the internet connection of the administrative office what type of internet connection are you using? When asked to respondents, mostly 76.25 % respondents said that the wireless or Wi-Fi connection is used in the administrative office whereas 21.25% respondents said to be used in the administration of the cables for the internet, while the lowest 2.5% respondents says the DSL internet connection in the administration today.

It is clear explain from the above information that in today's administration, the internet service seems to be time most used type of wireless or Wi-Fi that's why money is not wasted, it seen to be useful to everyone in today's administration.

Satisfaction in digital work

To study the satisfaction of the administrative office, are you satisfied with digital work in administration? When asked about this question, mostly 71.25% respondents said that we are satisfied with the digital service in the administrative offices whereas 27.5%respondents say that in administrative offices digital service is somewhat satisfied and the lowest 1.25 % respondents said that we are satisfied due to digital services in administration.

It is clear explained the above information that the digital service in the administrative offices are the best, so the peoples satisfied about administration administrative good. This service makes the administrative work even faster so that all the administrative employees are satisfied.

People's participation in administration

Does the People's participation in the administration? When asked about this question mostly 61.25% respondents that when the people's participated in the administration 38.75% Respondents said that the participation of the people's in the administration is in somewhat.

It is clear explained the study that while the administration was proving to be more involved in such a situation the participation of computer literate people in the administration is high and when uneducated people appear to be robbed, digital administration can be successful only if the administration officers and employees are required to provide digital service training.

Nature of people's participation

What nature of people's participation in public administration? When asked about this question, mostly 78.75% respondents are said to be getting service though citizen CSC, Aaplesarkar portal, and e-suvidha center etc. While 10 % respondents taking offices visit and participating in administration, when 8.75 % respondents contacted by mobile phone while getting participation in administration. Finally, the lowest 2.5% respondents said that we have use mobile apps and with participation in administration.

It is clear explain the above information the public participation in administration today is being seen by mostly services through CSC Apple sarkar, E-Suvidha facility center and some important tasks are seen in the completion of the administration with the help of this center.

Digital services in Administration

What is the maximum number of citizens who come to study digital services in administration? When asked about this question most 58.75% Respondents say that the citizen's office comes in various certificates. And also 16.25% respondents says that if ration cards come to the offices then 15 percent of respondents are coming to the office for get 7/12 (Satbara). And 75% respondents say that if the citizen comes to the office for avail the benefits of various government schemes, then the lowest 2.5% respondents say that they are also visiting the office for pay tax on various forms to various formats.

It is clear explained that most of the citizen appear to be coming to office for get the various certificates.

Work tension in Administration

For the study, about work tension in administration is the digital service less effective in administering work? When asked about this question, mostly 57.5% respondents say that the administrative work has reduced due to the digital services 42.5%respondents says that somewhat work tension has reduced in administration.

It is clear explain the fact that the administration tress has diminished due to the digital service, but due to the fact that service did not reduce the stresses due to the problem of using it the problem of Internet connection, website hacking, etc. increases the tension of the administration. The administration can perform well only if the administration is less stressed.

Reasons of decreased work tension

What is the reason for the administration to reduce the stress of administration if the tress of administration is reduced? When asked about this question mostly 55% respondents says that e-administration policy reduces the workload of administration, while 38.75% respondents says that the creation of their Government service centers reduces the workload of administration and 3.75% of respondents says that decreased work tension due to use of government mobile apps, then the lowest 2.5% respondents says that decreased work tension in administration due to the e- governance training.

It is clear explain that the reasons for the administration to reduce the stress are responsible however, the highest number of e-governance policy has resulted in various forms of alternative, according to CSC, Aaplesarkar, center, e-facilitation center, and today's citizens appear to be completing their work.

Frequency of digital service training

Regarding of digital service training a question has been asked, have you been trained in digital services? When 53.75 percent respondents say that we get training on digital services, 46.25% respondents say that no digital service training has been achieved, it shows that 53.75% of administrators have completed digital service training.

It is clear from research study this information that while training is provided in the digital services it is necessary that the benefits of those services reach the public. Today, under the guidance of digital India, the central government is training the officers by Indian Institute of public Administration (IIPA) while training for the administration of Maharashtra is given by YASHADA.

Benefits to citizens through digital service

What are the benefits of public services due to digital services? Question arc askcd to respondents for the study, 88.75% respondents says that the digital service helps save time, 11.25 % of respondents are nothing expresses opinions respondents does not react. While 86.5% respondents say that work saved, whereas 13.75 % of respondents do not react. 62.5% respondents say there is no political intervention in the administration, but 37.5 % of respondents do not react. But 100 % respondents say that digital services don't require bribes.

It proves that many benefits are made to the public through digital service, saving time, saving money, saving work and no bribe is given at any time and when officers and employees are also working responsibly.

Digital Administration need of hour

Do you think digital administrations becoming the need of the hour today? Such as question asked when to respondents for study when 96.25% respondents said that the need of the hour is now digital administration, while 3.75 percent respondents said that digital administrations is no need of hour.

It is clear that today; all the states of India are digitizing through the program of digital India, so that every government service rendered by the government is also in digital format like from birth to death all work is digitized. That's why this service is becoming a necessity for the time being, which will building our country transparent and development.

Need of digital administration requirement.

Though the question of whether the digital administration is becoming a necessity for today's time such as asked to respondents' to kind out the reason, 61.25 % of respondents says that by making government services online, India is becoming digital, to stay in the world championship, to create knowledge based society, while

38.75% respondent says that above all reasons not that their, but for to eradicate corruption, for transparency, to reduce the rounds of the office, to increase computing knowledge etc.

It is clear explain that digital administration is becoming a need of hour, digital administration is in needed for the creation of the most knowledge based society.

Reasons for getting administrative service nearly

Administrative services are getting in nearby places. Because:- such as asked question to respondent for study,61.25% respondents say that effective Implementation of e-governance policy, the creation of CSC, Aaple sarkar service Centre, Developed mobile apps. For reduce red tape etc. while 38.25% respondents say that there is no reason to get administrative service, other reasons the set up NIC Centre in Administrative offices like collector office sand sub divisional offices, due to the creation mobile government apps etc.

It is clear explain from the above information that the most import ants reason is that administrative services are being found in nearby place due to effective implementation of e- governance policy, digital services in Nanded district distinct.

Tools of public service delivery for citizens

What is the tool of public service delivery to citizen? Such as question asked to respondents for study, 58.43% respondents say that tools of public service delivery to citizen through the T.V. channel / newspaper, CSC / Aaple Sarkar service Centre, Government offices and mobile government etc. these tools used in digital services. While 41.57% respondents said that do not use the above tools in digital services to citizen. Nevertheless, the highest 76.25% respondents says that CSC is getting more services through its government service Centre, the lowest 41.25% respondents says that government services were provided through mobile government.

It is clear that most administrative services are being given by CSC / Apple starker Centre.

Difficulties in digital services

What are the difficulties in providing digital services for study, digital service issues? When asked about this question, 46.25%

respondent says that while providing digital services problems like disrupted power supply, Computer short coming, untrained staff, and unavailability of internet service etc. 53.75 % respondents say that there are no problems with this. Nevertheless, the highest 58.75% respondent says that various difficulties in digital services due to untrained staff in the administration. The lowest 35% says that Computer Shortages are problems.

It is clear that although there are many problems in providing digital services in the administration, today the digital services provided by the administration are getting the public quickly and getting the service without the agent, so we have save money, time and hard work.

Identification of Digital India Concept:

Do you know the concept of digital India that has selected whether the digital India concept is known to all? When 100% respondents asked about this question says that digital India knows the concept. Officers and employees of the administrative office in Nanded district found this concept to be known when the NDA regime came to power, this concept came into in to existence in 2015, though today it is known that all in office this concepts.

It is clear explain that all the officers & employees of the office are aware of the digital India concept, that our county is moving towards creating a knowledge based society. Today our country is known as digital India in the world.

Today the country's prime minister is building the world's identity and it is proud to be honored by many awards.

Impact of Digital India program on Administration

To study digital India's results, what impact did digital India have on digital administration? When asked about this question, 67.81 % respondents says that internet service reached in village, e-revolution was created, A knowledge based society in emerging etc. due to digital India program. 32.19% respondents say that of the digital India programs did not affect any of the above. Nevertheless the highest 91.25% respondents say that the biggest impact on administration due to the digital India program is that on the basis of knowledge based society creation, the lowest 85% respondents say that e-revolution was created.

It is clear that today our country is becoming Knowledge based society.

Components for the Development of Digital Administration

Which components are needed for digital Administration developments? When asked question to respondents for the study 63.12% respondents says that for the important component of development of digital administration:- digital literacy, High speed internet connection, mobile governance, Rural electrification etc. So, 36.88% respondent says that whey do not express any opinion about the above components. Never the less, the mostly 98.75% respondents says that the most important factor for the development of digital administration is digital literacy, while the lowest 26.25% respondents says that digital administration developed due to rural electrification.

It is clear explained that the above all factors will lead to the development of digital administration, but basic requirement is that today, digital service can't be provided with digital literacy. Today, for the growth of digital literacy across India, the Government is implementing skill India program by the CSC Center.

Impact of Digital Technology on health

What are the effects of digital technology on our health? When a question has been asked, 63.12% respondents says that eye troubles, irritability, does not sleep well etc. effects due to digital technology on health 56.88% respondent says that the above results are not affected.

Nevertheless, the highest 83.75% respondents say that irritability is a mostly impacted on health due to digital technology, while 10% respondents says that does not sleep well.

It is clear that daily work is being done using computer in every office of the country, so every employee is using digital technology as a some result of bad health effect, but most of the employees are irritated with the behavior of his employees and his daily activities are facing problems it seem that many employees are willing to commit suicide because of not having a daily work and family work matter.

Use of Direct Benefit Transfer (DBT) Service in Office

Is the direct benefit transfer method used for financial management in your office? Such a question is asked, 98.75% respondents says that to used direct benefit transfer method for the financial management of the office. 1.25% respondents says that use of direct benefit transfer is going on but all offices are not used, they are in process and will be completed in a few days.

It is clear that every offices in Nanded district is using for financial management system. The other think that is used with it is that transparency in the government offices using JAM. (Jan Dhan, Aadhar, Mobile.) in the past. Rajiv Gandhi said the only 20% Rupees reach out of 100 % Rupees to beneficiaries. But through this DBT, 100% of the money would be deposited in beneficiary accounts. It is seen that there is no leak and no need of agent, so there seem to be the benefits of digital administration in India, enables transfer of government benefits directly to the bank account of beneficiaries, led to the integration of 440 schemes and the disbursal of INR 7,33,981 crore, resulting in saving of INR 1,41,677 crore the number of transaction for financial year 2019-20 alone stands at 21 crore.

Advantages of Digital Services

How will the country benefit from digital administrative services? Such question asked, for study 69.69% respondents says that nation be develop, corruption will be free, will be Known as digital India, Transparent country will be created due to digital administration service, 30.31% respondents says that express the opinion that the above benefits are not being achieved. Nonetheless, 87.5 % respondents Says that the biggest advantage of the nation to digital administration services is the help of a transparent country will be created. The lowest 51.25% respondent says that nation will develop.

It is clear that today the biggest benefit of digital service will be for the creation of transparent India. Similarly, this will lead to the economic development of the country and every state and district of the country will be developed.

Profile of CSC / Aaple Sarkar, e-Suvidha facility Centre operators

From 80 usable samples, there were 73.75% male (59) and 26.25

female (21) respondents. Based on the analysis on the data it is clear that the number of male respondent is higher that female respondents.

The Participants were divided into five educational level majority of respondents come under 40% are graduate and 35% are post graduate degree 18.75 % are completed their higher secondary, 6.25 % are completed their secondary and primary is nil. Means are nil. Graduate and post gratuity topped in the respondents list, where very few respondents were from higher secondary and secondary and primary is nil. The overall study shows that the CSC and Aaple Sarkar. e-suvidha facility Centre should have gender and education to be the participants of digital services.

Most Useful Services through Digital Service

Which of the services do citizens avail of through their Digital services center? Such a question has been asked 51.04% respondents says that Aadhar service, education service, financial service, health service, Government scheme and various certificates/ licenses act. Services are mostly useful through digital services, 48.96 % respondent says that do not take benefit of this service. Nevertheless, the highest 82.5% respondents sys that come to get various certificates / license 68.75% respondents say that for comes to get government scheme, 71.25% says that for came to get only Aadhar services 40% respondents says that for come to get Educational service, and the lowest 68.25% respondent say that for come to get health service only

It is clear that coming to the digital service center to get the most different – different certificates & licenses that is why administration is transparent and prompt dynamic

Use of Banking System by Digital Service Center

What type of banking system do you use while offering digital payment services? Such a question has been asked, 55.31% respondents says that net / mobile banking, debit card create card Bhim apps and AEPS etc. use / the banking system. 44.59% respondents says that we do not use this banking services nevertheless, The highest 70% respondents says that we used net banking, mobile banking. While 66.25% respondents say that we use debit / Credit Card, 52.5% respondents say that we use Bhim apps and the lowest 32.5% respondents says that we use AEPS system.

It is clear that today digital payment is being used due to the demonetization in India digital service centers are also using this system when it comes to cashless India it is necessary to use digital payment towards. Today's many innovative digital payment, namely Bhim, UPI, Bhim – Aadhar, Bharat QR code. National electronic toll collections etc. have been implemented In India Digital payment transaction on UPI including Bhim – UPI has grown 8,000 times from October 2016 to March 2019.

Internet Connectivity in Digital Service Centre

Which types of internet connectivity in your digital service Centre? Such a question has been asked, most 71.25% respondents says that we have Wi-Fi and wireless connection available to us, after that 18.75 respondents says that we have DSL Connecting available to us the lowest 10% respondents says that whence only cable connection available to us and dial up connection is a very old that's why it cannot be used.

It is clear that today the Wi-Fi and wireless connection in the digital age are in very high use in digital era. Because of the high speed internet connection, saving money, hence the use of internet connectivity is increasing in all the digital service centers. Similar question were asked to officer and employees but the reply was similar to this.

Training of digital service

You have digital service training? Such a question has been asked, most 65% respondent says that we have trained, while 35% respondents says that we have not trained.

It is clear explain that the operator of CSC / Aaple Sarkar Center and e-Suvidha Centre are taken training about digital seva, but entire CSC / Aaple Sarkar Centre, e-suvidha Centre has not trained. Therefore, they need to training through the training all the activities of the CSC Center can be Completed Properly and can be provided. Today due to the absence of training, many issues have to be faced if the training is completed then all these problems can be solved, such digital training system is available in IIPA for central government officers and employees and state government of Maharashtra's officers and employees in YASHADA Pune and also NGO's etc.

Problems of digital services

What are the problems of your digital service center? Such as question asked for to study the issues of digital service center when most 72.5% respondents says that unavailability of internet service in CSC / Aaple Sarkar Centre, e- suvidha Centre, after that 18.75% respondent say that disrupted power supply in CSC / Aaple Sarkar Centre.

The lowest 8.75% respondents say that website hacked into our service centers. It is clear explain that many services have to be faced by the digital service center.

Which is the problem of the unavailability of internet services? and also disrupted power supply, website hacks etc. today, need of 5G internet services are available in our country for the resolution of these issues.

Digital service charges

What is the basis of the charges incurred by digital service Centre while serving them? Such a question has been asked, 100% respondent says that government rate are decided, 87.5% respondents says that individual moderate rate and 40% respondent say that nature of work is taken into consideration.

It is clear that, every CSC, Aple Sarkar Centre, Setu Suvidha center charges as per the governments' fixed rate while charging the fee, and also individual moderate rate taking by operator of CSC. Even when the service is being provided to the public by the CSC center, the additional charges are levied so that the farmers and the citizens were exploited and looted but should be 50% discount for senior citizen, former, students etc. therefore, in all the place the service charge should be the same.

Recognizing the India as a digital India.

What will our country are known in the world as a digital India? Such question has been asked 88.75% respondents says your country will be introduced in the world as a digital India due to digital India program, 11.25% respondents say that our country is not recognized as digital India in the word.

It is clear that in every state a CSC center is being created today every citizen of the country has reached digital service, so citizens can avail the service and not need go to the city. Through this saving time, money, work, as a result, its social, economic development and administration have diminished, so that one day our country will be recognized as digital India in the world.

Profile of citizen

Demographic Profiles of the respondents (citizens)

The following section will clearly explain the demographic details of the respondents who are participated in the survey. The demographic, profile is measured based upon their gender, Place, age, occupation, education level and income category which are listed out in table. 4.34

Place

From 120 usable sample, there were 72.5 % Urban (87) and rural (33) 27.5% respondents. Based on the analysis on the data it is clear that the number of urban respondents in higher than rural respondents.

Age

Majority of the respondents are from the younger generation between the age group 26.35 years with 38.33% there are only 35.% of the respondent between an age group of 36-45 and 19.16% were aged below 25 and there are only 7.5% were aged group 46-55 and nil percentage of respondents between an age group 56 above.

Gender

From 120 Sample, there were 73.33% male and 26.67% Female respondents. Based on the analysis on the data it is clear that the number of male respondents is higher than female respondents.

Occupation

The participants were divided into five occupation lave. Majority of the respondents come under 26.67% are students and 22.5% are employee, 20% are worker, 15.83% are self-employed and very few respondents come under 15% are farmer.

Education qualification

The participants were divided in to five educational levels. Majority of respondents come under 25% degree/ diploma and 22.5% are post graduate degree, 18.33% are illiterate, 17.75% are completed their primary & secondary, 16.66% are completed higher secondary education. Graduate and post graduate topped in the respondents list, where very few respondents were higher secondary education

Income

The participants were divided into five income levels, 33.33% of respondents have an annual income 10,000-25,000, 30% have an annual income of above 25-50 thousand and then 17.75% come under the category of BPL. Finally 12.5% have income 50 thousand to one lakh. About 6.66% are under 1 Lakh -above. The overall. Study shows that the citizens income most 10,000 to 25000.

Identification of Digital Administrative service

Do you know, what is digital administration? Such as question has been asked, for to study of identification of digital administration, 81.67% respondents says that we know about digital administration/ services, 18.33% respondents says that we does not know about digital administration.

It is clear explain that although this concept of digital administration is new, it seems to all, know all the citizens of India are availing the benefits of digital service. This service is providing to citizens to their homes, so that any work information is found in the nearest place and the work is being completed in time.

Use of Computer

Can you use of computer? Such as question has been asked for to study, 58.33% respondents says that we can use the computer, 41.67% respondents says that we cannot use the computer.

It is clear explain that today in the digital era everybody needs time to get access to the computer, but even today some people cannot use the computer so many problems arise in their work. Today digital India, skill India program is providing computer training to every person so that they are computer literate.

Use of Mobile phone

Which mobile phone do you use? Such as question has been asked for to study, 68.33% respondents says that we use smart mobile phones, 31.67% respondents say that we use simple/ basic mobile phone.

It is clear explain that today, in the digital era, smart phones are commonly used by all citizens. Because use for sending money, railway, bus reservation, mobile recharge, interaction with social media. Etc. through smart phone, every citizen is endeavoring to bring happiness to his life and administration work is also being done through the apps of this smart phone while every office department is making mobile phone and trying to serve them through it. That's why everyone uses Smartphone.

Place of Digital Services

Which place do you go to get digital services? Such as question has been asked, The highest 55.83% respondents says that we go to the CSC and Aaple Sarkar center, e- suvidha center, 22.25% respondents say that we use mobile apps to get digital services, 15% respondents say that we go to administrative offices to get digital services and the lowest 6.67% respondents say that we go to the agent because we don't understand about digital services.

It is clear explain that every citizen is getting a service through digital service center because of the fact that every service is being provided by digital service whereas agents are seen going to office, whereas young citizen are also taking mobile services using mobile apps, there was dynamism.

Benefits of digital services

What benefits do you get by digital service? Such as question has been asked, the highest 56.67% respondents say that we are saving money, time and work. 15.83% respondents says that apart from the agent, we are taking advantage of digital service, 27.5% respondents say that all information is available on the internet, there is no benefit, no one responded to this option.

It is clear that digital services have much advantage, most of which save work, time, money, and the information that we get from the internet gets instant access to it, no dependence on others, difficulties get delayed and timely work is completed in time.

Difficulties of Digital services

What are the difficulties when taking digital service? Such as question has been asked to respondents for study of difficulties in digital services. The highest 43.34 % respondents says that there is an unavailability of internet service while taking digital service, 37.5% respondents say that power supply breaks when taking of digital service, 7.5% respondent say that difficulties in digital administration due to computer shortages. Lowest 7.5% respondents say that untrained employees and computer language cause same difficulties in digital administration.

It is clear explain that many people are facing problems while taking advantage of digital administrative services which shows the internet unavailability, to solve this problem today, 5G Services have to be started right now immediately and need of hotspot services on very public place.

Highest digital services in the facilities center

Generally, what services do you take advantages of by digital services? Such as question has been asked, mostly 47.5% respondents say that taking advantage of the various certificates. 30% respondent say that take advantage of government schemes, 11.67% respondents says that take advantage of digital service to get 7/12 transcript, 7.5% respondents say that takes advantage of digital service to pay for various taxes. The lowest 3.33% respondent says that uses a digital service to get a license.

It is clear that while availing digital services, certification, and at the center to get the most different licenses. It is clear that in today's era, the citizen goes to the digital service center to get the various certificates when required everyone is going to digital service Centre.

Transparency in digital administration

What has been the transparency in administration due to the reduction of corruption by digital administration? Such as question has been asked, for the study of transparency in digital administration, 94.17% respondents say that reduced corruption and there was transparency in the administration. 5.83% respondents say that there is no transparency in administration due to digital service.

It is clear that today the services are being served through the digital service center throughout India, hence, the timing of file processing is completed and its work seems to be completed, which has resulted in transparency in administering administrative corruption and reducing corruption in the administration.

Earlier, since there was no offline office file, bribe was being sent to forward the file. Today the automated file is going on in process.

Respondents Opinion

1. For the success of digital administration: - 100% literacy, power supply, economic progress etc. are compulsory. After the financial progress from self-employed, digital life will be fast and meaning will be achieved.
2. The speed of the work has increased due to digital administration that's why government schemes are implemented effectively. There is a need to implement more and more digital administration at village level.
3. Remediation measure should be taken to eliminate employee's computer illiteracy and social illiteracy, so that digital administration can be implemented properly and beneficial.
4. The digital revolution has brought about a catalyzing the lines of ordinary people. A bigger example is the lives of ordinary people A bigger example is the mobile revolution. Today a big businessman of a rickshaw puller, as student and house wife is using mobile phones. Today many services can got on mobile phone that is why it does not have to stand in queue for any work. as remittances are now being done through mobile.
5. Given the use of Aadhar card, the beneficiaries are getting direct subsidy. So the government has saved thousands of Crores of rupees. It is made easy to deal with Bhim app, Rupee debit card, and e-correct. The life-saving plan has helped many elderly people to get pension and benefit from various government schemes. Due to digital schools, hospitals, rural people have reached this service.
6. There are advantages and disadvantage of each revolution there are also benefits and disadvantages of digital revolutions well. The new challenges like online scam, fraud and

cybercrime are being created due to this revolution that's why the government has taken several laws and measures for cyber security for the insurance sector universal development is the main purpose of the digital revolution India is going to be the world financial center by this development. This revolution has transformed the lives of ordinary people.

This revolution has made life easier for the common man keeping in mind the responsibility of digital revolution, this revolution will not take long to make human life beautiful.

According to the above study it is clear that the positive and negative view of the digital administration were selected respondents, and it has become clear that digital administrative service has become a cause of great happiness for every. Citizen's life, transparency in administration and not getting the scope of corruption, people are getting services. Also on the CSC Center and Aaple Sarkar Center, e-Suvidha Kendra creating jobs and also administrative work load reduced automatically. This digital administration will recognized the India known as digital India and will not have time to develop the nation.

Chapter - 5

Finding, Conclusion and Recommendations

Introduction

Providing of Digital services facility to citizen, from central and state Administration in Digital Era.Therefore, in every state digital service portals are being created by the administration today, like aapale sarakar centre (portal) setu suvidha in Maharashtra, me seva services in Telangana and Andhra pradesh. As well as providing services to the citizen through CSC centres across the country. That is why promoted the digital India Programme. This programme launched in 2015, for ensuring digital access, digital inclusion, bridging the digital divide and digital empowerment, leading to Indian's transformation into knowledge based economy and digitally empowered society.

The government is committed to provide governance and services to our citizens in an affordable and efficient manner within the shortest span of time. India sitting on the robust foundation of digital infrastructure and expanded digital access, is now poised for the next phase of growth creation of tremendous, economic value and empowerment of citizens as new digital applications permeate sector.

Ministry of electronics and Information Technology has recently released "Indian's Trillion Dollar digital opportunity" report to boost the scale, scope and digital innovation of citizen centric services, which can result in a jump in digital contribution to the Indian economy up to USD. 1Trillion by 2025, 9 specific areas have been identified for government interventions.

This chapter unfolds the finding of the research. This research offers possible relationship between the past studies and the present research findings. The importance of Digital administration in all public utility service platforms in India is clearly stressed in this study. After taking not from various literatures of government adoption studies, an analysed holistic the cortical model has been developed for both citizens and employees' intention to be use digital government system.

This research study also attempts to get the bright glimpse about the factors that facilitate the intention to use digital government services by common people and common service centres operators and employees in various revenue Department.

The conclusion and suggestion arising out of the study are presented, it was observed during the research material on related subject of the study and number of Areas.

Findings

Time researcher of this study has been considered it necessary and useful to also look at the Digital Administration phenomenon at the International, National as well as State level. The researcher has analysed the primary data to study the awareness of Digital Administration services implemented by central, state government as well as the view of the employees in revenue Department, CSC centre operators and common citizen's.

All the employee of revenue Department are educated, mostly graduate Degree Awarded and also all employee of venue Department have adequate Knowledge of computers with Internet literacy. Due the implementation of Digital administration and give better service to citizens by a saving their time, work, most of the employee in the offices are male graduates in the age group 28-37 year.

1. Today all sub Divisional offices of Nanded District have been found to have computerized with Internet connectivity. So the citizens are getting services immediately.
2. When the speed of the work in the administration was studied, it was found that 92.5 per cent of respondents say that there was mobility in the administration means administrative work is fast.

3. When studying how digital service effected on administration, 65 per cent respondents say there was transparency in administration. Today every sub Divisional office digital transparent. Due to Digital Administration.

4. All employee are using computer in Administration, it is found that 71.25 per cent employee using computer and other employee are use the tools like mobile, Laptop.

5. Advantages of the e-governance involve that the government may provide better service in terms of time, making government more efficient, transparent, responsive and more effective.

6. It is found that 76.25 per cent offices using Wi-Fi, wireless internet connectivity in administration

7. 71.25 per cent of a employee satisfied while using Digital services so his work is fast and prompt.

8. It is found that 61.25 per cent of people were participation in administration. Due to the digital administration so many people's will be watch on administration.

9. It is observes that78.75 per cent of peoples were participation in administration through CSC/Aapale sarkar centre, setu suvidha centre.

10. It is found that 58.75 per cent of citizens came to the administrative office for various certificates

11. Reduced administrative workload due to Digital service centre like CSC, Aaple sarkar centre, setusuvidha centre, etc. All peoples are getting Digital services through Mobile apps, that is why mostly employee's work tension were decreased.

12. 53.75 per cent of employee was got Digital service training through various government institutes. That means many employees are not trained. Due to lack of training cannot provide better services to citizens.

13. The benefits of Digital service were studied, 88.75 per cent employee said time, work saved. That is why administrative work is prompt.

14. Importance of Digital Administration were studied, 96.25 per cent employee says digital administration is today's Era "need of hour in Administration, because from birth to death all work is digitized.

15. Digital Administration 'need of hour' because 61.25 per cent employee says for creates knowledge based society, for To survive the global competition, and India towards to Digital India and also for online services.

16. Administrative service are getting in nearby places, because 83.75 per cent employee says that effective implementation of e-governance policy and 67.50 per cent employee said that creation of CSC, e-suvidha centre. It is found that Digital India & effective Implementation of e-governance policy that is why all Digital services are getting in nearby places.

17. Digital services problems were studied, 58.75 per cent of employees untrained and it is found various problems like Disrupted power supply, computed short coming, unavailability of Internet service etc, employees have to face those problems while working in administration.

18. All administrative officers and employees are aware of the 'Digital India' concept. That is why our country is towards creating a knowledge based society. Today our country is known as digital India in the world.

19. Development of digital administration were studied, it is found that 63.12 per cent of respondents said that, most important component in the development of Digital administration is digital literacy, after that High speed internet connection, mobile governance, rural electrification etc. That is why NDA Government is implementing skill India program and also various courses based on skill.

20. The Impact of Digital technology on health was studied, it is found that eye troubles, irritability, does not sleep well etc problems were in administrative staff therefore, high quality tools have to be used in administration.

21. It is found that in all offices are using Digital finance Management system, like Direct Benefit Transfer (DBT)

service, and also JAM etc. (Jan Dhan, Aadhar, Mobile) Due to DTB, 100 per cent of money would be deposited in beneficiary accounts.

22. How digital administration benefits the country when it was studied, 69.69 per cent respondents says that Nation will be develop, corruption will be free, will be known as digital India, it will help to create a transparent nation.
23. It is observed that 51.4 per cent of citizens say that Aadhar services, government scheme and various certificates, license etc. services are mostly useful through digital services centre.
24. 55.31 per cent Digital service centres, Net, Mobile Banking, debit/credit card, Bhim app and AEPS etc. using banking system mostly using Net banking by csc centre. Today Digital payment is being used due to the demonetization in India. Digital services centres are also using this system when it comes to cashless India it is necessary to use digital payment towards.
25. The operator of CSC, Digital trained, and services centres are taken training about digital services it is found 65 per cent of operators are trained and other 35 per cent operators has not trained, that why number of facing problem related of technical problems.
26. 72.5 per cent operator's says that unavailability of internet service in CSC and e-suvidha centre, after that disturbed power supply and also many problems creating while getting Digital service facility.
27. Every State Digital services centre providing digital service facility to citizens so, citizen can avail the service and not need go to the city. Through this saving time, money, work, as a result its social, economic development and administration have diminished, so that one day our country will be recognized as a digital India in the world.
28. 58.33 per cent citizen's says that we can use the computer, 41.67 citizens says that we cannot use the computer. So, many problems arise in their work. Today digital India, skill India programme is providing computer training to every person so that they are computer literature.

29. 68.33 per cent of citizens were found to be using smart mobile phones, while 31.67 per cent of citizens were found to be using simple mobile phones.
30. It is found that 55.83 per cent of the citizens were going to digital service centres for digital services other citizens going to administrative offices and agent and also using of Mobile apps for digital services.
31. Using digital services can save money, save time and save work and no agent needed, all information is available on internet. That is why no dependence on other.
32. It is found that, Disrupted power supply, unavailability of Internet service, untrained staff, and Computer shortage language etc. difficulties while getting Digital services. That is why many citizens are facing problems while getting advantage of digital administrative services.
33. It is found mostly found that 47.5 per cent of citizen going to digital services centres for the getting various certificate like, Domicile, Cast, Income, nationality etc. certificates other facilities 7/12 (Ultra), Government scheme, various tax, to get a licence etc., facilities getting on Digital services centre.
34. When transparency was studied in the administration, 97.17 per cent of the citizens said that there was transparency in the administration .Due to digital services hence the timing of file processing is completed that is why reducing corruption in the administration.

New Innovations Model

'Office connect' apps A Mobile tools for smart Administration

Description of Model:-

1. To create mobile application for each District included sub-Divisional.
2. There should be one mobile application for each Department of the District, like revenue health, agriculture, etc.
3. ID and password should be must to using for this application.

4. This should include arrangement for making payment, application to various scheme and also various services.
5. The next final process OTP or password has arrived from the relating office while serving on the Mobile application.
6. There should be a toll free number for SMS and calling if there are any complaints about this application.
7. Everyone must need to create an account in mention Aadhar number is compulsory while using mobile application. Because not to be misuse and fraud.

One Nation one platform services (ONOPF)

Description of Model:-

1. All ministries and Department of central Government under this platform.
2. Every state of Ministries and Department under the platform. (separate pocks for each state)
3. To create new account who are getting services and his linking Aadhar number and also linking of his mobile number because not to be misused and fraud.
4. All centrals and state government services can be access under one portal.

Other recommendation

1. Awareness programmes for e-governance application:- The Government can create awareness among the citizens employees using mass media, like namely radio, Television, Newspapers, Handbooks and public awareness program should be arranged highlighting the relevance of it in daily life like-Digital India programme.
2. Inclusion of computer, Education at school, college, level, all school and college level computer education is must because today's era, is Digital, every work is Digitized that is why all people students employees computer education is must. The government should also arranged, and subsidize. It vocational training to create and digital literate society with an awareness of e-governance application.

3. To increase digital literacy government can plan basic digital literacy courses for the common citizens like basic computer. MHT-CIT, Tally, C^{++} etc. such as a course creates by state, central government.

4. Supply of computers and laptop on subsidized rates to citizens, students, NGO'S. Most people in the rural areas however using the mobile phones now a day and have been very comfortable using the various functions. Computer literacy can be increased if rural people are encouraged to purchase the computers making it available to them at subsidized rate.

5. To strong Internet connectivity in all areas. Today's era is most important of internet connectivity in administrative offices and CSC. Aapale sarkar, e-suvidha facility centres and public place. Special connection-optical fibre, Jio, cable, likely internet is most importance in life every people. That is why they are need of hour, to the need of 5G internet for high speed internet.

6. Provision of Basic facilities in every offices and Digital services centres like, power supply (UPS) Annual Maintenance contract (AMC) essential spares and consumable assistance of trained hardware and software engineers.

7. Digital training program for officers, employees all state and central government and also various Institutes, NGO'S officers and employee's Digital training should be compulsory.

8. There are various successful corporate sponsored ICT based market placed in operation across India. Contributing positively to the rural development. One such successful ICT based program is e-choupal, an initiative of the Indian tobacco Company (ITC) limited, corporate may agree to provide necessary infrastructure facilities for implementation such programs as it would benefit their business interests. On the other hand, it can boost the government's e-governance initiative for rural development.

9. **Updating data base:-**

   There should also be process for day-today regular updating of data on every website; projects involve the storage and retrieval of huge amount of data.

10. **Administrative perspective:-** For effective implementation, an employee who is immune to change is needed. Psychological counselling. This counselling will clear their doubts and they may realize the importance of implementing new technologies.

11. Implementation of e- governance project improves the inter-relationship. Increases government and citizen and administration and administrative effectiveness and efficiency in government affairs. Encourage local software companies to take an active part in development.

12. To improve skill in cyber security, must need to introduce cyber security courses at school and college level and encourage inter nation, national certification bodies to introduce various skill based cyber security courses.

Bibliography

Books

1. A. K. Srinivas and other, *case studies on department of registration and stamp*: project sarita, NeG plan.
2. Aglave Pradeep, (2000). *Research Methodology science and technics*. Nagpur, vidya prakashan.
3. Arun Jaitlye, (Nov-2018) *a people's movement,* Article published in Yojana, government of India.
4. Shrinivas Raj, B. (2008). *E-Governance Technique*. New Delhi, New century publications.
5. Barotia G.R, sharma, K. (2002) *"Research Methodology*. Jaipur, Mangal deep publication.
6. Bharatwal, C.P. (2003*) good Governance in India*. New Delhi, Deep and Deep publication.
7. Chandra, Bhushansharma, (Dec 2018) *innovation in technology supported Distance learning,* published Articles in Kurukshetra Journal Gov. of India.
8. Malohtra, Charu. (2018). *Role of Digital Technologies in governance* New Delhi,. IIPA
9. Christopher, G. reddick. (2012), *Public Administration and information technology,* jones & Bartleft, Canada.
10. *Common service centres,* Ministry of electronics and information technology, government of India.
11. D5 Landon 2014:- loading digital government Gov. UK. UK. Government. 2014 (online-eBook)
12. Deshmuksh. R.N. (2010) *Aaple Nanded Zilha*. Nanded, Kalpana Prakashan.
13. Eapen k v, (2018), *Effective grievance redressal Hart of Good governance*. New Delhi, (Yojana journal.) Government of India
14. *E-governance policy initiatives* under Digital India, published report, Department of electronic and information technology, government of India.
15. Godbole, Madhav. (2003) Publication Accountability and Transparency the in operative of good governance.
16. Godhaji Sonar (2009) *Aapla Nanded Zilha*. Nanded, Sant Kripa Computers.

17. Heller, Nathom (2017*) Estonia*, the Digital Republic the New York.
18. Kothari C.R, (2004) *Research Methodology' methods and Techniques*. New Delhi, New age international publishers.
19. National Research Council (2007) *social security Administration electronic service provision a strategic Assessment*.
20. Ray, Omar. (2017) *Digital India program*. yojana (Marathi,) New Delhi, government of India,.
21. Pankaj S. (2000) *Electronic Governance*. New Delhi, A. P. H. Publishing Corporation.
22. Amit, Prakash. (26-02-2017). *Digital India needs to go local*. The Hindu.
23. Pranavmukul, *digilocker initiative record repository* of 24.13lakh does from 2013,the Indian express,dated-06.10.2017.
24. Prasad, Ravishankar. (Dec.2018), *Digital the aim of empowering*, Article Published in Yojana Journal, New Delhi, govt. of. India.
25. Mittal, Sanjeev. (Aug2017) *e-governance in rural India*. article in Kurukshetra Journal, Ministry of rural Development Gov. of India,
26. Dua, Seema (2016) *Digital India Opportunities & challenges*. two days international conference, dev. Samaj college for women, ferozepur, Punjab.
27. Sharma K.K. (Ed) Sandharbha Maharashtra intellectual book Bureau, Bhopal.
28. Tom Butler, Joseph feller, (2005) *Promoting knowledge sharing in government and non-government*. organization annual conference 29 June 2005 Florence lately.
29. Valuliya, K.S. (2015) *Research Methods in social science* Jaipu, paradise publisher.
30. Yashada, (2005) *Right to Information, Training program for the resource person reading material*. pune, Yashada,
31. Sari, Yogesh and other, (Feb-2018) *New India*. yojana journal, New Delhi, government of India.

Reports, Documents publication

1. Digital India framework- A training handbook Indian Institute of Public Administration, New Delhi-2018
2. Digital India, targeting inclusive growth, ASSOCHAM, New Delhi 2017
3. Economic survey of Maharashtra 2014- 15, Director of Economic and statistics, planning Department government of Maharashtra Mumbai.
4. e-governance policy initiatives under Digital India, Department of Electronic and Information Technology Government of India,2014
5. National E-governance plan, Department of electronics and Information technology, 2016.
6. Population census 2011, reports government of India New Delhi
7. Shrinivas Ghatage, case studies e-Governance, Department of electronics and information technology, government of India
8. State of E-governance in Maharashtra 2013, published by Directorate of IT, government of maharashtr,2013

JOURNALS AND MAGAZINES

1. Indian Journal of public administration, Indian Institute of public Administration, New Delhi
2. International Journal of Humanities and social science, online raijmr.com
3. Journal of economics and finance, online Journal, www.josrjournals.org
4. Kurukshetra, Publication Division, Ministry of information and Broadcasting-Government of India, New Delhi
5. Lokrajya, Directorate, General of Information and public relations Mantralaya, Mumbai.
6. Maharashtra a head, Directorate, General of Information and public relations Mantralaya, Mumbai
7. The Indian Journal of political science, Indian Political science Association, Meerut, UP
8. Yashmanthan, Yashada, Pune
9. Yojana, publication Division, Ministry of information and Broadcasting-Government of India, New Delhi.

Websites

1. D5, Landon 2014:- loading digital government Gov. UK. UK. Government. 2014 (online e-Book)
2. http://accenture.com/xdoc/10c/june 20,2007
3. http://digitalequality.in/history-of-governance in Maharashtra
4. http://google weblight.com/i2u= http://public Administration un.org/e gov kb/ en.us/ Report un.e-Gov.survy2018
5. http://india.gov.in /MPPS
6. http://meity.gov,in /division/national-e-governance plan
7. http://meity.gov.in/content/state -data-centre
8. http://nap. edu/read/11 920/chapter/11/# p20013
9. http://nesotencil:com/Smart-governance-inindia
10. http://nig.org/Knoeledgecentre-docs/A036604
11. http://www.drishtilas.com/UPSC-exam-gs-resources E-Governance m
12. http://www.insightsonindia.com
13. https/aaplesarkar.mahaonline.gov.in/en/commonform/atsact.
14. https://csc.gov.in /government to citizen.
15. https://csc.gov.in/Financial inclusion.
16. https://csc.gov.in/government to citizen.
17. https://edisnic.gov.in/dynanic administration.
18. https://m.nandedonline. in /city- guide/geography of Nanded.
19. https://mahabhulekh.maharashtra.gov.in.
20. https://mr.vikaspedia.in/e-governance/online citizen/services/92e93993e.
21. https://nanded.gov.in/subdivision-bloeks/-
22. https://Pmg disha.in/students/counts-list/

23. https://transformingIndia. My.gov.in/per form dashboard/primary
24. https://Vikaspedia.in /e-governance/e-district/mission mode project
25. https://vikaspedia.in/e governance/best practices/rahuri in ahemednager/first to have digilocker
26. https://webumang.gov.in/web/#
27. Maharashtra state e-Governance Report, 2014